LEARNING FROM OUR LIVES
PORTRAITS OF CONTEMPORARY WOMEN CLERGY

Anum Akai

First Edition

ISBN-978-0-578-74176-5

Library of Congress Control Number: 2020914345

Dedication

To the eight women clergy who gave their time and shared with me great stories of their lives before and after seminary education. Also, Theo, Lynette, and Noel Akai iv

Acknowledgement
Thanks to God and all those who in various ways
contributed to the completion of this book:
Dr. Chere Gibson, Jerry Rodgers and Roy Lembcke

Table of Contents

Rev. Maurine, in her early sixties, is the rector of an Episco-pal church in Mid-Western town, serving her seventh year. Prior to her appointment, Rev. Maurine served as staff cler-gyperson at a cathedral in Kansas and functioned as an as-sistant priest in a small church in California. Rev. Maurine engages in a variety of learning experiences that enables her to integrate her secular and spiritual lives which informs her professional practices. She defines learning as self-reinven-tion and reflection in action.

Rev. Martha, the Caucasian priest of a large Episcopalian Church in a Midwestern town, was a news reporter prior to entering ordained ministry. "I am the director of an Episcopal Church in downtown... In the secular world I would be con-sidered CEO of a company." Prior to coming to this church, she was the priest in charge of the Cathedral in Maine and thereafter became the Associate Dean. Before, she worked as an assistant priest at a small church on Maine's coast. Rev. Martha enhances learning from suffering, and some reflec-tion on past action.

Rev. Pat, the Hispanic Missioner of an Episcopal Church in a Midwestern town, develops children's ministry particular-ly with five-year-olds at risk. Later, she began teaching En-glish-as-a-second language. Rev. Pat, originally a Catholic in her late fifties, expresses familiarity with many cultures and speaks passionately about her ministry with Hispanics. She has an undergraduate degree in psychology and master's degree in nursing. Starting as a nurse and working in Bo-livia, she believes learning for professional practice occurs through balancing of self, and community action.

Rev. Pharmer, pastor of a small, low income, Lutheran congregation in a Midwestern town, works integrally with the community. She has adopted two children from the Caribbean. Rev. Pharmer is a Caucasian in her mid-fifties, and her first call was in North Dakota with a congregation on the Canadian border. Rev. Pharmer went to a convent near Dubuque and later to a private College. Before becoming ordained, she was a Roman Catholic sister. Rev. Pharmer defines learning as interior reflection, and communion with God.

Rev. Lin Grace serves as co-pastor of a Presbyterian Church for the past four months. New to this Midwestern congregation, Rev. Lin Grace is a Caucasian in her mid-forties. She served a church in Bridgehampton, on Long Island for five years before pastoring a congregation in crisis in Bernardsville, New Jersey. Rev. Lin Grace started working at 14. She worked with the Glendale YMCA as teacher for developmentally challenged children. Rev. Lin Grace learns through spiritual connection with God and others; she reflects in action, and she balances-self-care with physical activity and recreation.

Rev. Clara, pastor in her early fifties of a Presbyterian Church in the Midwest, oversees a congregation of three hundred members. Seven years as co-pastor, she became the solo pastor at the church. Rev. Clara had no role models for women ministers during childhood. Her decision to become a minister was influenced by her college friends. She learns through motherhood, small group relationships, and from the stories and struggles of church members. She seeks self-renewal through focus on God, and feeling God's presence.

Rev. Bonnie, pastor at United Church of Christ, located at the southwestern end of a Midwestern town. Rev. Bonnie is a Caucasian, in her late fifties. She has traveled extensively to Europe, Asia, and the Middle East. Before she came to this church, she worked as the associate conference minister for United Church of Christ. Her responsibilities included women's issues, outreach ministry, and education. Rev. Bonnie has a master's degree in guidance and counseling. Rev. Bonnie learns through global awareness, visualization of places in the Holy Land and experience of God's presence, and connecting with people.

Rev. Bethke, pastor of a Methodist Church in south-central Midwestern town, was a district superintendent, responsible for 50 churches. She served eight years as the lead pastor in Oshkosh. Also, she served eight years as chaplain at a Methodist retirement center. Rev. Bethke, in her early fifties, has a degree in nursing. Her undergraduate work led her toward towards nursing, one of two options at that time, nursing and teaching. Rev. Bethke learns by gaining distance from material objects to see God more clearly.

Introduction

This book is an empirical guide for ministry and Christian living designed for women clergy, seminary students, and laity. It tells the story about the learning experiences of eight women clergy during and after their studies in various theological institutions and up to their call to full time parish ministry. In an unstable, Post-postmodern era, characterized by diminishing notions of reality and *truth*, perceptions of life's meaning seem fragmented and subjective. Thus, religion is pushed to the peripheries. The outcome of this shift creates a divide between sacred and secular lives. This book empowers clergywomen to reconcile their secular and spiritual lives, which accordingly informs their professional practices. Also, the book enables these women to meet the demands of their clergy roles so they could live balanced Christian lives. Both women and men of the clergy can learn from those pastors whose ministry learning experiences are presented in this book. Female clergy across a variety of religious traditions are a likely audience for this book.

Our contemporary Society is changing as secular life becomes more sophisticated. Adults become more sophisticated in actions and thoughts. In response, people develop complex lifestyles, and secular life detaches from spiritual essence. As Apple (2001) states, "The love of money, and the accumulation of capital, has led to the steady decay of religion. Religion had lost its moral significance because it did not touch on matters economic, except in the most tangential way" (p. 24). Advancing technology's instantaneous availability of information on every subject (via internet) brings significant change in social and religious systems. This new information age carries with it the notion of sound bites. Society's perception of what is whole, such as

information, has been reduced to smaller segments for easy marketability and assimilation. A sense of incompleteness spurs us to move toward fulfillment. Our sense of immediate reality compels us to spend greater portions of our lives addressing complexities. As a result, "We have to learn to think differently, not just do different things . . . we have to move, flow, dance, recognize the instability of everything including cherished notions of career or profession" (Clarke & Newman, 2001, p. 44.). People now express their senses of the past, the present, the future, their destinies, and their senses of self in terms of this new milieu-information age (Dimitriadis & McCarthy, 2001). Remarkably:
These new mentalities and self-imaging are driven forward by an ever-expanding sense of possibility—as well as terror and constraint—as modern humanity cultivates new interest needs, desires and fears in the landscape of the new [culture] . . . New critical discourses have been generated to address the challenges of the new age. (p. 2)

Over the years, women have been known for their strong resilience in the face of challenging circumstances. For instance, women continue to seek a proper place in a society where they were in past alienated; whereas those who feel called and enter ministry may have to deal with a second dilemma, which is finding refuge within a vocation that at one time, was male oriented.

Relatively new to parish ministry, women clergy demonstrate innovative ideas and ways of doing ministry by virtue of their unique faith encounters, within a former male oriented institution. Portraits of eight women clergy and their stories permeate this book. These stories, based on a series of interviews, serve as a vehicle through which they perceive the world and their ministry. Stories provide insights about how women clergy's experiences enable them to construct meaning that informs their professional practices and helps them meet the demands of their spiritual and secular lives.

CHAPTER ONE
Pastor Maurine

Maurine serves as the rector of an Episcopal church in a Midwestern town. In her early sixties, the Caucasian rector begins describing her role in the church. "I'm the rector of St Dunstan's church or senior pastor, and I have been here seven years or more. I was called here to do this, so this is the only role I have had in this church". Prior to her appointment, Maurine served as staff clergyperson at a cathedral in Kansas and functioned as an assistant priest in a small church in California. Also, she worked as a parish administrator. "Everyone has a story about making the decision to enter seminary and become ordained," Maurine asserted. Certainly, she also has a story and it happened in Dallas. "Women were beginning to be ordained to the priesthood in our denomination but not in Dallas . . . and yet things kept happening, and I thought well, maybe I need to...." So, Maurine had to leave her hometown Dallas and become ordained somewhere else.

And...that wasn't ...'cause they didn't have any there... I got sort of popped out of the process in Dallas, the ordination process, but I had already been accepted at a seminary so, I called the seminary and said: 'What do we do?' . . .she said, "Well you're not the first person this has happened to and you won't be the last one so come on,"

Later Maurine graduated from a seminary in the West Coast and was ordained in the Diocese of El Camino Real.

Learning Experience in Secular Roles
Maurine holds both bachelors and master's degrees in English with specialization in linguistics. She explains why she focused in linguistics: "I did those things in preparation to teach ESL (English as a second language) before it was its own discipline. They were using linguistics to teach ESL. Yeah, so, then I got started on a doctorate in literary translation, and God got my attention. So then I went to seminary. And I had thought I would want to do that for preaching, get a PhD to teach preachers. I was married for sixteen years to a physically abusive man, I said it was for keeps, I'm not a quitter. But I finally got out, and we all started to get well. I have three children and they each have a spouse and I have five grandchildren." Maurine talks about relationship with her grown up children. "My oldest son and his wife and child are coming to visit this week. Well, they are great. It's great to have children, have your children grow up enough to be your friend. Though, I'm not responsible for them anymore, I take their advice and sometimes they take mine. Yeah, it's good".

Before her seminary education, Maurine held various positions in both the public and private sector. At 37 years old, she worked in the research and development unit of Texas Instrument, a big corporation in Dallas.

I went to seminary from a big corporation called Texas

Instruments in Dallas where I was at that time working in   research and development organization doing inter viewing and writing for people for that organization. And before that I had been in a training department as a trainer and then as a designer of trainers, for training, and then as a manager of training designers, so it was all teaching. Well, I was at Texas Instruments seven years, and I was in the public schools one year as a teacher of English as a Second Language and one year in a subset of a school district that was mostly African Americans, and I was dialectologist. I was working with dialects and helping teachers work with dialects, yeah, so that's what I do….

These experiences broaden her outlook about life and work. Teaching is the common element in her secular life. So, one might say she becomes a… "Researcher", "trainer" "designer of training" "manager of training designers", and "ESL teacher", but she feels "it was all teaching, it's always something; mostly it's been something to do with teaching. And even in research when helping people pull documents together, I was teaching English…."

Maurine discuses a critical learning experience in her secular life that informs her daily life and reflects on those occasions where learning occurs. She remembers too well the story about her learning experiences at Texas Instruments regarding her involvement   with staff training programs… "for newcomers on how to make outsiders not feel outsiders and that has been transferable in the church… I pull it out of corporate America. It takes some thought to fit somebody into the community. And so, I'm all the time looking for what they like to do…." For Maurine, this means deeper knowledge and understanding of the context within which church members function. More so, it's about adaptation of learning experiences from a corporate setting into the sacred domain. She insists the church must also show hospitality to its members especially those who are newcomers. "You know you come to this church to visit and it's like falling into a box of puppies. They're all over you, and licking you, and loving you-just wonderful. But it takes some thought to fit somebody into the community. And so I'm all the time looking for what they like to do. What does their ministry look like? And then, finding the right people for the new person."

Another critical learning experience that informs her professional life is "reading novels, which sound fairly superficial, but I think I have learned a lot about human motivation and human behavior. Because a good writer is spot on about why people do what they do." This reflects her academic background in English.

Overwhelmed with her new sense of vocation for ministry, Maurine describes her experience in the process of making the decision to enter seminary. Here, learning manifests through sustained self-awareness. "I, you know... Not bragging, I'm a five-talent person. God has dropped a bucket on my head, of the talents that I have are about persuasion, creating space, and all the things that the priest needs to do. So, those talents paid off!"

 Learning also occurs as she experiences a sense of divine awareness and utilizes poetic discourse to express her faith. "I had to leave home and family to do it, but I did it. Jump off the cliff, says God, I'll catch you! And I learned that God really does catch you when you jump off the cliff." Maurine leans on God for divine guidance as the decision to enter seminary became daunting, "I know how frightened the church is …I learned that people will support you until the going gets rough. You really find out whom."

Learning Experience in Relationships
In seminary, Maurine discovers her greatest experience in
learning through relationships. "I always wondered why
our new curates would just disappear for couple of days
cause somebody halfway across the country was getting
ordained or installed or something. You make relationships
in seminary that are worth a million dollars I just had wonderful teachers.... I learned there will be friends in unlikely
places." She seems particularly interested in making friend-
ships because some friends could bring healing and com-
fort in times of distress. She speaks of a troubling incident
when she newly arrives at the seminary.

> ... I came to seminary, and of course, you know, you
> sit in the dining room and everybody says, 'Where are
> you from? Which diocese are you from?' And I would
> say, I don't have a diocese. Dallas is not friendly toward
> any woman. So that went on... I was honest about it.
> And that went on for a couple or three days, and then
> I met with my faculty advisor, who said 'Don't tell
> people your situation because they're all scared to
> death it's gonna happen to them.' And I said, well
> you're too late, I've already told them and all that
> happened was that my classmates just gathered. They
> healed me from that awful state.

Maurine expresses her sense of human finitude, probably as
a way of overcoming those uneasy moments in seminary.
"You know; seminarians are human beings just like everybody else but in a sense they're people who are trying to be
good in a way that may be some others aren't".

She also has friends with whom she develops various learning relationships that inform her daily life. She welcomes the relationships she develops which prove purposeful and intended to bring about specific learning outcomes. In some situations, Maurine befriends individuals who are experts in specific fields, a process which enhances learning. For instance, her first friend was a woman from San Diego, who before seminary, had been a therapist. "And oh, we could talk about anything." So, learning emerges as they explore various issues and topics. She has another friend who is cathedral priest. She describes some of these learning relationships...

> Then I made friend, good friend with a man who was fresh into seminary from a Tibetan Buddhist monastery. And, we had a lot of talks about different kinds of religions. And that was just a richer knowledge of course. And friend, I'm still a friend with them. I did a long retreat on the west coast in January and stayed for three nights with another seminary friend who's doing wonderful creative things in Carmel, California. Uh, she helped me design my ordination, because she's so artistic and creative. She's a bit younger than I am, but I think maybe that's something that can happen when you come to seminary... You know, you're more of an age group.

Here Maurine suggests that a diversity of peers in seminary was an important resource for learning.

Learning Experience in Spiritual Roles
After seminary, Maurine continues to learn and communicates her aspirations for lifelong education. "I believe that heaven will be a different place. I hope I never in eternity quit learning. Our denomination says, 'you must have in your contract continuing education money. Expect to learn

every year'. So I've done preaching workshops, I've done workshops of a particular size, in the parish that I'm in, and how to deal with that." Participation in continuing education programs fulfills her educational needs, increases her learning experiences, and improves her professional practices. In this learning process, she and her peers nurture one another toward professional growth.

Maurine feels fortunate to have participated in a workshop organized by Rabbi Ed Friedman who "has taken family systems' theory and applied it to congregations as a family system." What she learns from this workshop is one concept the facilitator projects, "Leadership is not about what you do, and it's about who you are. I mean from right here (referring to the heart)." For Maurine this learning experience has been… "One of the most useful things, one of the most useful concepts that I have ever…and I tell that to parishes, and they sort of looked puzzled like they don't get it. But then if they've watched it for a while, they see why it works." Maurine literally immerses herself in what she learns, and that learning process becomes part of her being and leads to self-reinventing. "Concerned with growing up people of God," and not anxious about growing numbers in the church.

Maurine believes learning experiences necessary to accomplish a specific learning outcome may take years. "And we have something going on called Church Development Institute which we have just signed up for. Two of my parishioners will be going to that for the next two years. So that's something else I've learned. I always …always belong to a group". Also, she identifies group learning as a method from which new learning experiences emerge. "I always… I always belong to a group. So, I'm always learning." It is interesting to observe that Maurine did not belong to one group. Similar to her approach toward relationships in seminary, she belongs to various peer groups whose activities through different levels of interaction brought about significant learning experiences. ". . . I got here, and I was addicted quilter, making quilts, well, there is wool, so I have learned to knit, and I'm an addicted knitter now."

She reveals that learning sometimes occurs informally, involves risk taking and can be a painful process. She speaks about her temporary new role as the president of the board of the diocese and this experience shrivels her soul for a while.

> Last year, I didn't do any continuing ed., per se, our previous bishop took a medical retirement, and I was president of the board of the diocese, and the buck stopped here. And that was some of the most painful, and some of the most grueling learning I have ever done in my life, was trying to care for what this place needs, care for 62 parishes. It shriveled my soul for a while . . . and then once we elected a new bishop it was my job to be as much to help him, you know, insert himself in the system as I could do. So, I was in a position of having to help someone, but I really didn't feel... Well, I've come just to adore him. Uh, I see that he is the most useful person we could have right now, but that was a hard thing to do.

Maurine sees learning as a passion driven activity so each time she encounters a new learning situation, a sense of fascination arises and subsequently leads to reinvention of self. She uses the terms 'learning' and 'passion' interchangeably. "I have just started a new passion and that's hiking and camping. So, I keep reinventing myself. And I keep learning new things and having new passions" Certainly, she continues to involve in other kinds of learning experiences that lead to learning in her life. And these experiences are not always directly related to church programs. "And I've learned to grow orchids up here, and I've learned to grow antique roses up here, and I'm learning to grow—I've never gardened in my whole life, I kill things." As learning emerges through interaction with different learning groups, she constructs meaning from these experiences.

Gardening conveys a deeper meaning for her. "These people have taught me gardening, and it's another new thing to love. So, I learn about church and I learn about God and I learn about God's world I learn about making new things." Maurine presents another significant learning experience that helps her meet the demands of her spiritual life. "The man who had this parish was the interim, not the rector but the interim priest who did an absolutely wonderful job… the expectation was that you couldn't have known when he slept, and I found myself falling into that…" In this experience Maurine learns that "death is nature's way of telling you to slow down." She asks rhetorically, "How does anybody have time to check in with the creator? You're always tending to others." She confronts a seemingly conventional wisdom that portrays pastors as professionals who ought to work all day and all night. "So, I began just guarding my day off like a mother tiger. I've always have known that you have to have your own friends outside the parish." This means developing networks within and outside the parish. She differentiates between being a buddy to some people and a priest to others. "You can either be their buddy or their priest, but you can't be both. And so, that's one of the reasons I got into orchids and roses; there are societies for those things. I have friends in those societies, and I wanted friends that were not even clergy in other churches. I have met clergymen who have friends who are absolutely not involved in the church." But at the same time, she has clergy friends with whom she is "able to talk about spirituality, but we won't have to talk about church politics. And that has taught me about love your neighbor as yourself. First you must love yourself before you can love your neighbor. So, I've just been loving myself". Maurine perceives her professional role in the light of a holistic life style. "I don't always want to have to live out of the role of the priest... she and I, are able to lay that aside and just talk about our children, experiences of humanity, of the wildflowers here and the trees there."

Maurine reacts to learning experiences that helps her meet the demands of her spiritual life. "Yeah self-care is pro— how does anybody have time to check in with the creator, you're always tending to others. You know, you do hear God's voice through your parishioners and I certainly listen to them. ... But you must be, you have to shut up and listen for a while." She finds her spiritual essence in this process of silence and listening. "I take three days of silence a quarter. So, I can just gear down, so... I can remember who I am and whose I am. So, taking that time I think is, is what absolutely is essential for my spiritual life." Certainly, self-care in this context leans more toward spiritual sustenance. For her, learning experiences that develop a deeper sense of spirituality should not only come from colleagues or fellow Christians but through one's own initiative.

Maurine identifies a bewildering situation in her professional practice and describes how she learns to prepare herself for such spiritual life encounter. She refers to an interim pastor deposed from the parish because of an inappropriate relationship with a parishioner. "...No longer a priest because he got involved with a parishioner, and there was a sexual relationship. It usually takes a parish about ten years to recover from that kind of situation. And Patrick came in and was an interim pastor, which means mopping up the blood you know and doing the first step things." She considers her role in this adverse situation as the "after pastor", and her responsibility was to "teach people that lies and secrets and silence are a bad idea, and that boundaries are a good thing. And, that's a kind of doing ministry that I have never done before, but I have done a lot of work around sexual ethics. And so, with a lot of coaching, and grieving and talking. That's what I came here to do." Maurine recognizes the "only way you can do that is not by doing, you can't do it by doing, you have to do it by being who you are… you have to live in a goldfish bowl so that you have nothing to hide." Her challenge is to help people say, "Well, she's not perfect, but I trust her. So that's been the challenge, is to be transparent, is to work at being just open."

In responding to ways which her faith helps in creating learning experiences towards her personal and spiritual lives, she speaks specifically about sermon preparation and emphasize the complexity of this learning experience. "Oh… every Sunday, I go home, and I read the lessons for the next week and on very rare occasions the sermon just kind of blossoms. Most of the time it's like Jacob wrestling with the angel and it's tough, and look at him and I think I don't like that." However, Maurine understands that "wrestling with giving people a word week after week after week is some of the hardest and most fruitful spiritual exercise I do, is preparing to preach. And I write two sermons a week, one for Sunday and one for Thursday."

Integrating Secular and Spiritual Learning Experiences in Parish Ministry

Maurine invokes the word "balance" to articulate the learning experience that helps her integrate both her spiritual and secular lives to meet the demands of her professional roles. "We talked about balance already; taking time for yourself and taking care of yourself." Alluding further to integration, she explains, "women don't compartmentalize spiritual and secular … as usually as men do. There is no part of my life that isn't spiritual." She argues that both the Eucharistic bread and wine are holy. "Because all bread is holy, because all wine is holy everything God has made is holy. I get up and put food in the dog bowls and it's a holy act." She believes when she sits down with her knitting that was a holy act because she prays while she knits. ". . . but again, integration is like water for a fish, 'cause everything is sacred. Everything is part of God's world. Integration is not even on the screen for me, it's just all there." At the same time, Maurine agrees and asserts that advancement in our society has led to the creation of both secular and sacred domains. She believes the secular world will do everything it can to try to make you believe that. "And sometimes, you get sucked in a little way and then you have to remember who you are and get back out." She thinks the extent of integration or disintegration of secular and sacred lives depends on the spiritual maturity of the priest. But, as she points out, it is sometimes difficult to discern one's spiritual maturity.

> There is nothing that can show you, really, how healthy somebody's spiritual life is. ... the only thing I think of that can show is when the heat is on …see how they perform under pressure. Whether they demonstrate their faith or whether they demonstrate their fear

She expresses frustrations with the use of some electronic gadgets. "I gave my Palm Pilot away last night, I'm sick of it. I'm going back to a book." Then she describes how centering her life enabled her to manage this movement between the secular and sacred. "Three days a quarter in which I get silent and I get my boundaries back. And that's the truth. I come out of that three days and I'm myself again, I'm back. And that'll last, and then, stop short again, and say "Whup! Time to get centered again" So, four times a year without fail…" Maurine describes her moment of silence.

> I go up on a Sunday night. I turn off the computer, I turn off the TV, I turn off the radio where all my classical music, even I turn off my grandmother's clock which chimes. And it's just me, and God, for three days. And I usually start out with this whole big long list of things I could get done, and then I get up on that morning. And so, I generally, get the hymnal out, and leaf through it, until a hymn chooses me, and I pray the hymn. And it has a benefit of having learned a new hymn by heart. But it also gives me a prayer, a lovely prayer that I can use for three days. So that's what my three days… except sometimes I will make the music, I have recorders… sometimes I make my own music. And of course, I talk to the dogs. But . . . I don't talk to another human being, and I don't hear another human being. You know, you're just bombarded with information, and chatter, and stuff all the time.

One example about secular lifestyle that caught Maurine's attention was the use of technological gadgets. She uses this example to express how integrating secular and spiritual lives can bring about learning and professional growth. "I have my cell phone. It helps me become available to people. And, I've done some, some pretty good pastoring on my cell phone. I think I have done some pretty good pastoring on the Internet with email. I'm on a list server for knitters. And they got into a conversation one time about, "My preacher doesn't like it when I want to knit in church."

And so, they asked me, "What's your take on this?" I don't know, I think I gave a good answer. So, I find it very useful"

Even with those electronic gadgets that seem to be nuisances for her use, she affirms how helpful and important it could be for some of her colleagues. "I was talking this morning at breakfast to the woman that I stayed with last night who uses Palm Pilot all the time." She speaks about how this woman and another colleague find the Palm Pilot helpful.

> Well, the bishop and I both use them and they're useful because the person who keeps our calendars can feed them into her computer and we always know where the other one is. That's wonderful help for two extremely busy people who are taking care of a tremendous number of parishes and some terrible political garbage. So... that's useful for doing God's work. I think you don't let it lead you around by the nose. I'm grateful for dishwash ers, microwaves, cell phones etc.

She explains how integration of her spiritual and secular lives influences how she learns. As a loving child of God, she becomes more patient with herself. Maurine believes there are physical limitations and doesn't have to…

> be responsible for everything. I don't push myself as hard as I used to because, God didn't die to leave me in charge and other people had skills and gifts and I get to leave cookies on the plate for other people." She believes in keeping an open mind. When she encounters people, whose opinions are different from her and "try to understand where they come from.

Learning Opportunities and Professional Growth as Influenced by Gender and Position

Maurine responds to a question about how her gender and position have influenced her learning opportunities and professional growth. "Well, I remember when I moved to Kansas, to serve the cathedral. The bishop let me talk to another woman cleric of the diocese. And I said, 'How is it for women here?' 'And she said', 'Well, it's a boy's game, but they'll let you play'. And that was a kind of "stained glass ceiling". She believes things have changed. "It seems although it's been propped up some, you know women are doing things in the church now that there are deans and bishops you know and that's fine."

She further explains her views on gender and position as it relates to her experience. "Gender and position as I say after last year vastly expanded my learning opportunities into areas that I didn't particularly want to learn anything about. . . I can go to any kind of continuing education program I choose." Maurine now feels the issue is not much about gender. Perhaps she was envisioning the physical challenges that will face her in the years to come considering she was nearing retirement. "What's influencing me now more currently is not my gender but it's my age. . . I passed sixty, although I must work here until I'm 72. So, that for me now is my concern." She speaks well of the bishops in the diocese because they support women ordination. "Now women are a very strength in this diocese . . . the new bishop likes that a lot. He's much more collegial and collaborative."

When asked whether her role as a female clergy helps her in some way, she said "I don't think it has greased any skids for me. I don't think it's made anything easier. In some ways it's made things harder, although I will say, I think the search committee in this parish decided if we get a woman rector, she'll be controllable, - biddable. You don't get through the ordination process without having back-bone. And they were unpleasantly surprised that 'Maurine' sometimes stood up and said, "No, I don't think so," about something or, "Yes, we are gonna do this."

Maurine shares uniqueness about her ministry. "Well I told you about ten times, and it was only thing that made any sense for me, given my gifts, given my spirituality I guess it doesn't mean that in everything I am perfect." Evidently, her faith enables her to survive during times when women remain unwelcomed in parish ministry "but every time I thought, oh, this is a bad idea, the diocese of Dallas doesn't want you anyway." Somebody would come along and support her. "So, I just, I kept, just putting one foot in front of the other, taking the next step I saw to take. She felt this learning experience brought about growth. But, this recalls her assertion that the extent of one's spiritual health is determined when the heat is on. "I don't think you can do that kind of a thing if... it'll either grow you or kill you. And I'm still alive."

She believes learning also occurs through role modeling but feels such learning opportunity may not always be available. "I wasn't one of the first women ordained. I was may be the second or third wave. But still, particularly in dioceses where women were not welcome, you would be ordained and there were no models. How do I be a woman that does this when I don't see any other women do this? And, you would just glom on to anybody who could tell you how they made it work, you know . . ." She shares her experience on modeling.

Now, when I'm in with somebody because I remember their modeling for me, particularly, telling embarrassing things that it would have been my instinct just to shut up and it ended up being that's the right thing to do… she was running for bishop last year and she said, "You need to know that if you elect me as a bishop, you're gonna have a bishop who's dating so,. . . you know, other people might not have said that. That's what she is. And more and more, I'm learning to do that. And I remember another woman modeling to me…a positive attitude. I thought I was trying to see the upside and the downside of everything but in comparison to her…

Maurine sometimes does things in her way "which may look different from how Dave and John are doing it …that's not how I can do it, Okay. I must do it my way…when I baptize babies and, I go down the row and sit with the child that's brand new, and I'll bless them, just ruffle some hair… and that's just the mom in me, right, you know.

Maurine engages in a variety of learning experiences that enables her to integrate her secular and spiritual lives which informs her professional practices. She defines learning as self-reinvention and reflection in action.

CHAPTER TWO
Pastor Martha

Martha holds office on the second floor of a large Episcopalian Church overlooking a Midwestern down town capitol building. She was a news reporter prior to entering ordained ministry, and thus, shows lots of excitement and interest in this interview. Martha appears compassionate, and demonstrates great sense of humor. "I am the director of an Episcopal Church in downtown… In the secular world I would be considered CEO of a company. This Church situation is applicable because we have a budget of $450,000 closer to $500,000, and much of that money goes to our ministries." Within the Episcopalian tradition, her official title would have been Rector of the Episcopal Church, but she uses the title "Director" as a way of drawing a parallel between her church position and one that exists in the secular world. In her early fifties Martha, comes to this job a year ago from the Cathedral in Portland, Maine and expresses how difficult the search process has been. "It was about a two-year search in coming to an agreement with this church about them wanting me to be here." Before coming to this church, she was the priest in charge of the Cathedral in Maine and thereafter became the Associate

Dean. Before that, Martha served in a small church as an assistant priest on the coast of Maine…"and so those would be the three ordained positions I've held."

In college Martha majored in dairy science, swine nutrition and sheep management. "After my education in agriculture I worked for the Associated Press which is a news gathering organization, and I was a political reporter, a crime reporter, an editor, and yes, that's about it." She worked for 17 years and then something unusual begins to happen. "I had a number of friends die, and my job as a news reporter was beginning to feel hollow, and my job as a reporter was to get up every day and find the worst that one human being had done to another and then write about it." Martha feels she needed an assurance so she "…could be in a job that offered more to my neighborhood and community, and that sort of led one thing to another, and I ended up in the seminary."

Learning Experience in Secular Roles
The work in the news business brings Martha into contact with people from different walks of life. "Through my work in the news business I experienced many of these people who grieve over death of someone or loss of their job or some criminal act they have committed. And those are my learning experiences." An emotional learning experience raising her awareness of…"trying to find out what value a spiritual community could be in the secular world." Martha speaks about a critical learning experience in her secular life that informs her daily life. "I do a lot of work with rescue dogs who are abused. The one lying next to you is an abused dog. Working with abused dogs reinforces for me how cruel people can be, how cruel people can be to animals and children, and the neglect they can suffer and the abuse." Through this experience, Martha becomes "even

more determined to watch out for little kids who may be in risky situations and try to find homes for dogs and cats that have been severely mistreated, yeah."

Learning Experience in Spiritual Roles
During Martha's ordination, "it became clear to the people who worked with me and to myself that I wanted to run a church." With this affirmation, her "learning experience largely became how to understand corporate worships, how to meet needs of most people in worship service, and to better understand group dynamics within the church." She recalls an incident that led to a great learning experience in her life. When she was seven years old, her father, an airplane pilot, died in a plane crash. Her family did not handle his death very well or tell her much about her father when he died, "we just quit talking about him." This emotional experience set her on a "lifelong path of wanting to know more about how other people experience tragedy in their lives and recover from it and become whole. Even at seven, thinking 'Why did my family handle this so badly and where are the people? And what do they have to say, who can help me get over this?'"

Martha shares another significant learning experience and explains how this experience helps her meet the demands of her spiritual life. "I have a tendency to rush and probably when you play this tape back, you'll say 'oh, she talks way too fast.'" She often rushes through life, which caused her to fall down on the ice some few years ago in Maine, a significant learning experience. "I mean I hurt myself because I was rushing, not paying attention, hadn't been to prayer that morning, and approaching the age of 50. Feels like God just stopping me and saying 'you have got to live your life more quietly, more slowly, you have to make time to see when you're rushing into something stupid like you

did today.' Accidents have most often affected my prayer
life more than anything else."

Martha reflects on a puzzling situation in her professional
practice and explains how she learns to prepare herself for
this encounter. She laments that women in the Episcopal
Church are a relatively new phenomenon, "it's only been
30 years that they've been ordained," and that can sometimes be a problem. "Episcopal women, women parishioners, some of them tend to want to see me as a friend and
they don't understand the professional boundaries and they
tend to want more of me than I can give. If it's not handled
very carefully and clearly, it can really end up with hurt
feelings on the part of the parishioner who thinks I just
don't want to spend time with them." Martha recalls a
similar recurring incident for which a priest in Maine finds
a solution.

> I learned to prepare for such an encounter because they
> happen numerous times… a very good boss in Maine
> who was good priest, and he gave me the language to
> help a person see early why I wasn't going to be over at
> their house all the time or going to dinner with them all
> the time or at movies all the time, and he helped me
> identify how to deal with a person early rather than
> getting upset with them out of frustration, yeah.

She insists we create our joy and that the bad things that
happen to us happen. "Most times we can't control something negative that is about to happen to us" For Martha,
creating joy as a learning experience toward spiritual fulfillment often comes through designing inspiring worship service. "One part of the Christian church that I'm determined
to build up is that we come to church to worship God we
come to church to praise God and Jesus". She thinks too

much of the church's emphasis on feeling of guilt or bad or small or unworthy, amount to an insult to God. "I think the more we feel bad about ourselves, the more we insult God who made us and right now we're in the season of Lent, and that's one of the reasons for Lent; to really focus on where you are sinful and fallen, have a contrite heart, exhibit remorse, make amends, and get on with it but not spend 12 months of the year remaining." Martha emphasizes the importance of healthy spiritual life.

> We have to get on with our praise and our worship. I mean, this world is so in need of good spirit and good healing and good joy and happiness that I wish people and the church would focus more on how we get to that which aids the building of God's kingdom. …I have a strong belief bad stuff happens to us, we can't control it, but we can control where we're going to have joy. We can make joy in ourselves and in each other.

Integrating Secular and Spiritual Learning Experiences for Parish Ministry

Martha talks about learning experience, which helps integrate her spiritual and secular life to meet the demands of clergy roles. She faces a physical limitation when she falls on the ice a few years ago. "I think of it as a midlife opportunity and not a midlife crisis." The fall was an "opportunity to really say 'you're not getting any younger, you have to let yourself be more vulnerable with the people in the church,' and it's been really lovely because it has allowed me to be exactly who I am rather than portraying who I hope to be which I used to do when I was younger. She maintains, "…it makes it much nicer for the people, too, because they're really clear on who I am and they're not seeing some kind of a portrayal of me."

Martha explains how integrating her secular and spiritual lives influences her learning as a professional clergy.

> Well, I see the Holy Spirit in most everything. I see Jesus' teachings in most everything and the power of God's spirit in most everything, so it's really my spiritual life that has influenced my secular life. I have a real love of the simple things in gardening. I have two worm farms. They make great soil. I have lots of worms, as odd as that sounds, and bees.

Martha uses God's creation to explain how one's secular and spiritual lives interweave. "When you go back to the very beginning elements of nature and see the beginning of God's creation, the bee on the flower, the worm in the soil, feeding the flower or making better soil for the flower, you see the hand of God is in literally everything. So, my secular and spiritual life is really nicely combined in my secular life and involves so much of the admiration of creation."

Martha provides new insights about her views on both spiritual and secular lives. "I feel that my spiritual life, in the hope of praying unceasingly, is with me even when I'm on vacation. The difference I think you're trying to get at is on vacation, I can do whatever I want and sort of follow a voice of God or look at something or stare as long as I want to at a painting on vacation." In church, Martha does not seem to be on her own. "When I'm in church I am at the beck and call of the parishioners, my time is not my own for the most part because I have a huge list of demands and needs that I have to meet on the part of the church. Both of them to me can be spiritual, working in the church and going on vacation." She explains further differences between spiritual and secular lives.

I can do whatever I want with my time, and I usually choose to use it in some quiet spiritual way or I can be in the church, which is where I'm working and serving others. The secular world, I guess I have the time to serve myself yeah, and in the church, I use my time to serve others. I would say I tend to be a sensualist, some body who enjoys textures of fabric, nice soft coats of dogs, feeding squirrels in the backyard. That is my secular life.

Martha reflects how her secular life informs her spiritual life. "That informs it in two ways negatively and positively. The negatively is I could spend all my time doing that, pet-ting dogs and looking at flowers and serving only myself. I could spend all my time doing that. I love to serve my-self. That's the negative side of it is you can really become very selfish with your secular time." On the positive note, she speaks about how her secular life informs her spiritual life or "integrates with it because I bring my appreciation of colors to the church and spirituality. I bring my appre-ciation of caring for the least of God's creatures from my secular life of rescuing dogs and cats into caring for the least of God's creatures, promoting that within the church." She brings much of her secular life experience into the church. "I can take a look at the ways I serve myself in my secular life and say many of those are really worthy things and I'm going to bring them into sermons, I'm going to talk about what happened to me last week in my garden. So, my secular life does integrate and inform my spiritual, yeah."

Martha responds to how technology helps her integrate both her secular and spiritual lives to meet her clergy roles. "Email is my big one right now. I don't know what I would do without email. It was finally how you and I got in touch with each other or how I got in touch with you because God knows you've been trying for three months to get in touch with me." She asserts technology should serve the people, but doesn't "believe people should serve technology; and technology has really become a deity, a god in our society, where people say 'I sent you an email and therefore that means you have to answer me. There's so much with cell phone technology and voice mail and email and all the realm of computers…we really need to take a step back from it and say 'is it serving us or have we become slaves to it?' I think we really have to keep in perspective the Biblical admonition of not making false gods"

In Martha's view, the secular world offers great learning opportunities. Some bring meaning to life, and some do not. "I don't believe in spending much time on focusing on what I can't change. I believe in accepting the world as it is, but I still believe the Bible applies to how we use our time, especially in relationship to each other's. If we really don't pay attention to our spiritual lives and the effect the secular world can have on it, then we are in danger of becoming slaves to false gods, yeah." The secular world sometimes weighs so much on her that she has learned to survive:

Okay, the secular frankly, I had tendencies toward this, but it's turned me into a hermit. I shut off my home, I don't look at my email, oftentimes I don't answer my door because the demands of my job are many, and to have the strength and peace of mind to do what I have to do every day, I need to make sure that my spiritual life is in shape and that I can wake up in the morning and be renewed and come back into the church and continue to do all the things I have to do. So, I do find especially as I get older and have less stamina, that I really have limited my secular activities because the world is stimulus overload and I'm like a crow. If I see something shiny, I want to pay attention to it. I want to be entertained all the time. So, I have to really shut myself away. People say I shut myself away more than I should, but I am very happy at home playing with dogs and gardening, yeah.

Learning Opportunities and Professional Growth as Influenced by Gender and Position

Martha recalls how her early formative years help her serve in male roles. While she was very young, even as a teenager, she worked in a man's world. "My first hobby or vocation or job was my family has a ranch in California and I was around horses. It's primarily men who do the work of cowboys, but my father had no sons. My father had four daughters, and so we did a lot of the work on the ranch that men would do."

So, she grew "…up aware that" she did things that girls didn't usually do. "But it was just the way the circumstances were." As a reporter, she did things that women don't usually do, but men do, and … "so I was a woman in a largely man's field." She describes a similar experience when she becomes a priest, "I once again was a woman in a man's field. I think the statistics right now is there is one-woman priest for every seven men priests. So, yeah, one in seven, maybe a little bit more but not much. So, that was something I had to live with all of my life and really didn't pay attention to people when they said, 'I don't know if a woman can do this' or whatever, I would just sort of go 'oh well, we'll see." She did not experience female-male relationship as oppressive…

As I know other women or other of my colleagues have. They experienced being in a male-dominated field as being very oppressive to them and to me I already knew how to be around men, work with men and get along, and it was fine…I am in touch with men every day who have nothing." These men belong to the church's home less shelter… "and they keep me in touch with how grateful I am for what I have, yeah.

Martha reflects on her encounters with parishioners.

I had one man say to me 'I won't take Communion from you, I won't let you bury me, I wouldn't want you to marry my children or baptize my grandchildren, but you're still my priest and I really like you'. I said, 'okay, that's fine.' By the time I had finished my work at that church with him, he said to me, 'Okay, I've changed my mind.' Essentially, he was saying 'you are legitimate, you are my priest,' and yeah. I don't often try to convince people theologically to go to a place where they aren't going to end up on their own. I really believe that I am here regardless of some-body's politics or theology. I am here to help them better identify the gifts they have in which they can serve God. That is my role. How can I help you identify your gifts to serve God? So, I really try to keep my politics out of it, yeah.

As a child advocate, Martha discusses her learning experi-ences with children. "I don't think we spend nearly enough time looking at what we have to learn from children or what we have to regain from children that we experience. I spend a great deal of time with the kids here in the church and in my secular life, too, and someone once said to me, 'Oh, you treat them as equals' and I said, 'No, I treat them as peers.' That, I think, is a big one. Go somewhere, be in the presence of a child and really listen to what the child has to say to you, yeah."

She believes understanding the underprivileged through the lens of their lives' stories is a great learning experience. She maintains learning emerges when we take responsibility for our part in the world.

> I mean taking ownership for the good things we do, pat ourselves on the back, and for the unconscious things we do such as buy clothes from third world countries where we get the clothes for $20 and some child or woman or man got slave wages for making them. I think we would learn exponentially and benefit if we just turned around and looked at our brethren in other countries and said 'that man is me, that woman is me, that child is me.' We are all of one blood, we're all of one blood, and to a great extent we all are brother's keepers.

Finally, Martha speaks about one of her church's mission projects "Because I see God's hand in most everything and running, having a shelter run from here, I am in touch with men every day who have nothing and they keep me in touch with how grateful I am for what I have.

Martha enhances learning from suffering, and some reflection on past action.

CHAPTER THREE
Pastor Pat

Pat, the Hispanic Missioner of an Episcopal Church in a Midwestern town, develops and coordinates children's ministry particularly with five-year- olds at risk. Later, she taught English-as-a-second language. Pat starts this job while serving as the associate rector at St Andrews and considers her associate rector position as full time. "You know; they were paying me three quarters' time. But it became more and more of a job that I was doing first on my free time, and then to basically redevelop this ministry from that which had been here in the past but had stopped being here. And what that initially meant was I did Bible study and outreach through the food pantry." She talks about her routine on a particular day. "We had Tuesday mornings we had different kinds of food and different kinds of hospitality to the people, because of the language barrier. And then I did vacation Bible school with the children, for a couple years…downstairs, while they were waiting and things like that."

Learning Experience in Secular Roles
Pat, originally a Catholic in her late fifties, expresses famil-

iarity with many cultures and speaks passionately about her ministry with Hispanics. She has an undergraduate degree in psychology and master's degree in nursing. Starting as a nurse and working in Bolivia for a short time, she returns to the States.   But, Pat considers herself as an educator. "I was basically, a staff development nursing educator. I did very little hospital work. I did some, but mostly, I was a teacher of other nurses, developing programs. And I would say that I did staff development for over 20 years but in different places. Yeah, I did it at Mendota, I did it for the University, for a five-year grant. I did it in a variety of positions." She claims learning occurs through community involvement. "Also, I've been on some committees in the community. I've lived in this community 30 years, so I know a lot of people. I really actually do know a lot of people, so that makes it easier for me to be credible in this community. A lot of people know me…I know that I should be willing to leave and go wherever, but I feel as though it's best for me to use what strengths that I have." Pat explains learning through connections. "My former Bishop, he said, 'Use your connections.' You know, and I do. And I have a lot of connections in the health community through the hospital, all that work I did at Merriter, I had worked there as a nurse, too. I'd say that's the main thing that I've done. I haven't done a lot of politics, per se. I'm not on those kinds of committees."

Learning Experience in Transition

Pat speaks about transition from chaplaincy to seminary. "I also felt that doing the work as a chaplain basically helped me to make the transition from thinking like a nurse in a hospital situation or hospice to paying attention to the spiritual needs which I felt was missing." As a nurse chaplain, Pat considers her relationship with people very important.

"I mean, I didn't tell them I was a nurse, for the most part; but I told the nurses sometimes, because that got their attention more quickly if I thought they needed to come quick. But, you know, for the most part, I feel that it was the reaction—it was the relationship with the people, and then the fact that, I didn't feel like God would let it go, I mean, I had to keep…It's the gospel story, you know"

In addition, Pat learns through self-awareness and argues with herself as she constructs meaning. "I feel like I'm a person of great privilege, because I'm…. I'm in this country, within a nice city, with a husband who of 31 years has no big problems. I mean he has a nice job and a nice salary. He's doing what he likes to do; and so, I can take this job for half time, and it's not a strain on our house or life, I mean it's OK. So, in a sense, having raised the family, I'm sort of done with the level of activities -which takes a lot of time and energy…you know, money. And we've done with that. Nobody is in college... At one point, four of us during one semester, all of us were in college at the same time". Pat argues. "My argument was, church doesn't need another 50-something, you know, white woman. I mean we needed to be looking at minorities. We needed to be looking at people; people with language…. 'You have another language,' is the answer I got back. Well, wait a minute. So, you know, at this point, my goal is to build this position into something that someone could move into when I'm ready to retire."

The six units of clinical pastoral education at Meriter Hospital greatly influenced her learning at seminary. It broadened her vision about connecting with people. As a chaplain, she encountered many people who did not have church. "'Do you have a pastor?' would be my first question. 'Is there someone I should call?' 'Oh no', I said,

"well…" So, I was it. I was the one if they were going
to have any chance of connecting … reconnecting….
These were all Americans—you know, born here—who
would honestly say, 'I am a Christian. I believe in God.
I'm a Christian. But I don't have a church. I don't go to
church. I say my prayers'. "Well, what kind of prayers?"
You know, I'd answer, "Well, tell me what…" It might be
something as simple as "Now I Lay Me Down to Sleep."
It was as complex …I mean, there's a range of types
of prayer that people did on their own but they had no
church."

Pat feels inspired by her relationship with people who
had no church. They contribute to her self-awareness."-
So that, for me, was eye-opening, because that said to
me, "There's enough missionary work to do right here in
the County. I don't need to leave town—you know, to
go somewhere else." There're all of these people dying,
and looking to somebody like me. So, to me that was a
life-changing experience. Yes, and that happened before I
went to seminary. When I was in seminary, all I was doing was reading books, writing papers, and running back
and forth from my home town to Chicago". Pat was not
on campus most of the time and that may have minimized
her seminary learning experiences. "You know, there
was no time to get involved in activities in the seminary
because I was leaving every weekend, you know. I… I
didn't even go out to eat sometimes—you know, to do
anything but read all those books and take all those classes."

Apparently, Pat experiences learning more during her
clinical pastoral education program than at seminary… "It
was in CPE (Clinical Pastoral Education) … Remember,
I did six units. I did that for two and a half years. I did

that longer than I went to seminary. It was in CPE that I realized that I had to stop thinking like a scientist, like a nurse, and open up my heart…I grew up Catholic, you know, for so many years; and Catholics are particularly, I think, poor at praying from their heart." However, Pat explains a critical learning experience at seminary. "One student called our liturgy team together at the end of the daily Eucharist and said, 'I need the liturgy team (A) to come and talk to me right now'. So, we all went—20 of us. And she said, 'I have to preach for the first time….' She was a woman from Kansas. She said, 'I have to preach for the first time on Tuesday, and I can't do that if you don't pray for me.' And we all stood there and laid hands on her and prayed for her, right in the in the aisle … in the seminary chapel. And that's the only time…. That's the only time in two years that anyone in that seminary asked for that kind of prayer and got…I mean she got it. And of course, we would do it, but nobody…No… Not once did a seminary professor pray with me. They would pray at the beginning of the class…I mean usually. But, when you'd meet with them or go to them with problems…Well, we had a chaplain. The chaplain would."

Pat considers learning at Seabury Seminary as formal. "When I was at Seabury I didn't find it a very prayerful place, although we were in chapel all the time. I mean, you could be in chapel for Morning Prayer, for eleven fifteen Eucharist, for evening prayer, for experimental Eucharist … dah, dah, dah, dah, dah. You know, it was all learning how to do the formal stuff. But the informal stuff—the prayer of the heart, I think, was kind of absent." She does not find seminary all that formative "because they don't let you do much on altar. I mean you're basically not much more than acolyte…So you didn't get a

sense to try on what it would feel like to be a priest deacon in the seminary situation."

Learning Experience in Spiritual Roles

Pat lives out her learning experiences and shares with
others. "'Pre-prayer' was a brand-new experience for me
in the Episcopal Church. And I've taught a lot of people
how to do that through the adult formation courses that I
did for three years at St. Andrews. But they weren't comfortable, because many of them were coming in from the
Roman church or from other traditions in the Episcopal
Church. So, this was something I learned how to do in the
Episcopal Church, and more profoundly through CPE—
how to do theology on your feet, for what was happening
right then and there." Pat discusses her learning experiences after seminary and how she continues to learn in
relation to her career, and begins learning how to read and
write in Spanish. "Could I do theology in Spanish? Could
I write the papers, understand the process, etc.? So, I did
that first, read not only religious literature, theology in
Spanish, I'd take some journals and I'd try to read them in
Spanish. I also have a tutor now. For me now, it's kind of
a problem—you know those details. Just paragraphs with
no changes at all. Praise the Lord! But sometimes this
looks like a Christmas tree with little red marks all over
it!" She describes this learning process.

> I use a red pen, and.... So, in that sense, I am trying
> to continue to improve all the time. I know how
> annoying it is if people are making stupid little
> mistakes up there in the pulpit. So, that's helpful to
> me to have someone, once a week for one hour, to
> just talk in Spanish. And she's not a member of the
> congregation,

so I can just say whatever I need to say. Yah, I got her
off the Internet. I got her off the University website
for the Spanish Department. I really think…. I pay
her well, you know, and so she loves it. In the summer,
we've been sitting down at Memorial Union.
Reading is another method by which Pat learns. She
bought a lot of books that she did not have time to read
in seminary, so she has those books all over her house.
"And I do read them, you know, when I'm doing sermon
preparation. I mean, I go back and I say, 'Oh, yah. I know
where there's something on this or that.' Pat continues to
learn through continuing education programs. "I did go
to a…continuing education program for the clergy, and I
did go to my church conference in Virginia. I actually got
some new ideas, and came back and implemented them
right away in the congregation. And people were all for
it. I have seven as far as continuing ed., that's about as
much as I could say that I've done." She believes the most
important thing is to realize that;

You're a lifelong learner, and that you never know.
I just never know. I had an experience not long ago,
where I was reading the Gospel, and during the
service.
And I had a whole sermon already written and
corrected in Spanish and everything else, and I stood
up and I said, "You know, sometimes it happens that
when I read the Gospel, it's as if I'm reading it for
the first time." And I have a brand-new thought about
it that I didn't write down; and I'm gonna give it to
you right then and there, and this happens when we
allow the action of the Holy Spirit.

. . . "Feels like I needed to share that so people would
know that these things do happen that you are learning

all the time, and that scripture is a teacher, and the liturgy is a teacher and we teach one another about ministry and about faith and about the presence of God. I think that that's one of the strengths of the Episcopal church—you know, that ability to be open and … and hospitable and welcoming to a variety of points of view—I mean, that you could have. You could be extremely Evangelical and conservative, or very liberal in your theology and co-exist"

Pat talks about an especially significant learning experience that helps her meet the demands of her spiritual life: "The biggest challenge for me is, if you haven't already figured it out.… I take on a lot. Even I could see that I was in over my head. You know. And so, there was not enough time, and I was working all the time. I wasn't.… Spiritually, it was an awakening to say, 'Wait a minute.' You know, 'I'm only one person. I can only do so much.' She weighed the situation with the hope of finding a resolution.

I had to discern that, because I was in pretty deep over there. I mean I had quite an active good ministry going. Four times—four separate times, starting August a year ago, I said, 'I think I'm going to have to go.' And he didn't hear me. And so, he finally said, 'Are you going to put that on paper—in writing?' You know, I said.… I had to write it down and give it to him, you know. So, it was a good ministry—what I was doing; but it was not good for me spiritually. I was not centered enough.

Pat explains an encounter in the church that informs her spiritual life. "I.… the rector wasn't there, and I went to the secretary to get keys to the church building. You know, it was like.… And she wouldn't do it. I called the senior warden, and I said…So, she said oh. So she did. But it took me, like a week to get a key to the church office. You know, which I thought…I don't think that would have happened to a guy. I just don't think it would have happened to a guy. You know, it was the kind of thing I had read about, you know—but never had experienced as a nurse, because we're all women … mostly. You know. I mean, everyone I worked with in the School of Nursing, for the most part, I expect being treated with respect. I thought that was disrespectful. There are things that continue to happen." Pat thinks out loud and hopes for survival. "It impedes you, I would say that was something subtle, but very hostile…How important am I? What does humility mean? What does it mean to be assertive, when necessary to get the job done? I've had a spiritual director since I was in the process, before ordination" She draws on her learning experience in psychology as a way of coming to terms with the issue.

> And what I know from psychology is that intermittent reinforcement…. You never know when you're going to have a problem, and if it's intermittent…. You know, if it's consistent, then you'll avoid something. If the person is friendly and sometimes they're passive or aggressive…. This really went on almost up until I left. For three and a half years it got a little better. I took her out to lunch. I talked about reconciliation. How I learn is trying to read people's responses. I had some training in this area as a psychiatric nurse.

Integrating Secular and Spiritual Learning Experiences for Parish Ministry

Pat speaks about learning through balance. "Finding your balance, finding your limits, to me has always been a challenge personally and spiritually. Making time to…. I have a practice of centering prayer, but I also like to go and meet

with the ladies who meet at noon on Tuesdays and do centering prayer, but we do it together." She explains further:

> I would say that would be the biggest challenge, I'm not
> done with it. While I'm on the phone, I'm folding bulletins.
> I have to be careful you know how many things I will say
> that I will do. I'm going…. Today…. I go court
> about—or to jail, you know, every other week. I'm
> going to court today with somebody. It's a different kind
> of ministry; it's an inner-city ministry. It's not like St.
> Andrew's, which a suburban. So, finding a balance
> personally is just a big challenge. And I think it is for
> clergy anyway.

Learning Opportunities and Professional Growth as Influenced by Gender and Position

Pat reflects on how gender and position influence her learning
opportunities and professional growth:

> Five classes and committees; I don't think that's impeded
> my ability to be asked to lead…And he said, "Go to the
> church planning conference." I think that there are still
> plenty of parishes that wouldn't hire a woman. You
> know, Martha's the first woman rector of this church
> since it ever started, and that was in '58. And so, they've
> had women associates and women deacons before and
> they're taking to it, as far as I can see. It makes them
> happy so, in that sense, I think things are still changing.
> It takes a lot of stamina I mean we take a lot of grief.

Pat shares insights about women. "Well, I think women are
pretty good at collaboration, anyway. Yah, women are pretty good at working as team members. One of my jobs was
to fly to Indianapolis with three other parishioners on model

of working together and rising up people for ministry.

Pat claims learning for professional practice occurs through balancing of self and community action.

CHAPTER FOUR
Pastor Pharmer

Pharmer, pastor of a small, poor, Lutheran congregation in a Midwestern town, works integrally with the community. "It's clearly poor . . . and works very, very integrally with the community of lower income… but they're committed to paying me the guidelines of the Synod, so I really appreciate that, it's a stretch". A Caucasian, she adopts two children from the Caribbean, which affirms the vision and goals of the church's ministry. In her mid-fifties, and 8 years with this congregation, she seems welcoming and very active in ministry. "This is my third call. I was pastor of a Lutheran Church, which is on the north side of town, for seven years before I came here, and my first call was in North Dakota in a congregation right on the Canadian border of North Dakota and Canada, and I was there for three years. I was the first woman pastor of that church." Ordained in 1988.

Learning Experience in Secular Roles
Pharmer studied at convent near Dubuque and later attended a private College, which was under the jurisdiction of convent community. So, she was in College in the 1960s when this college town had political turmoil, but she ap-

preciated that era. Before becoming ordained, she was a Roman Catholic sister who taught in the Catholic school system in Chicago and another Midwestern town. "The only time that I had a position that was not either connected with the Roman Catholic Church or the Lutheran Church was when I was a director of an alternative school in a Midwestern town for women. Mostly, I shouldn't say it was for women. There were mostly women, people who wanted a high school diploma and also people who needed to be tutored in reading before they could get their high school diploma." Also, she worked for the Office on the Aging in this Midwestern town, and interviewed elderly folks who wanted Meals on Wheels. In all she spent about 14 years in other fields of work before entering seminary.

Pharmer describes a critical learning experience in her secular life that informs her daily life. Her children in public school face "racism of the school system, and of individual teachers and that's a great learning experience. I think this town considers itself a very liberal community, and it is very, very difficult to be a person of color in this community. That has been a constant challenge." Pharmer responds to this challenge in a positive way, "I've done work in the schools where my children have attended on a personal level with teachers but also tried to do group work. It's just been really hard. It's been really hard."

Pharmer discusses the different types of experiences that lead to learning in her life. She describes how she learns greatly from other people.

> For example, in the early 1980s, I did a lot of work in Milwaukee with Salvadoran folks who were coming through the civil war in El Salvador and, and learned more about Nicaragua and that Central American experience

and really, they were my evangelists. They were people who taught me what it means to see poverty and injustice through the eyes of faith, particularly the women, I mean, they taught me through their stories and through their faith reflections.

She explains her learning experience in South America. "I spent some time in Nicaragua in the 1980's that was when the Sandinistas were just becoming organizing as the government. I saw Daniel Ortega sign the constitution that was a magnificent moment. To see that movement of the people came through... to be taught by people who had a different culture, economics, language...That's really significant." Pharmer also speaks about her learning experiences with the women she encounters when as the alternative school director. "They were mostly women who were much older than me. I was probably in mid-30s at the time. Many of them were grandmothers. They hadn't had high school education. They worked at very low-paying factory jobs, and they really instructed me on what it's like. Most of them were white, so that was also a real instruction."

There were those women, college graduates and teachers, from whom she learns many things as well. "These women taught me what it was like to have the kind of financial, or lack of financial resources, often in abusive relationships. And so, they really were my teachers." She reinforces what she learns from these people. "I learned from these different groups of folks and then I would go do reading or I would take a class or I would do a workshop. So, my learning always comes from connections with people and then I'd go to try and figure out, you know, how that happened and what the underlying background is behind that."

Learning Experience in Transitions

Pharmer recalls continual involvement with different aspects of the church's life. She taught in the Catholic school system, worked at Cook County jail, connected with the Roman Catholic Church. Also, she organized retreats with high school students. "So, I always did different kinds of ministry, but I just considered it volunteer work. I didn't consider it ministry, and it really came about when I moved from Chicago to Milwaukee, and in the Milwaukee Roman Catholic Church, there was no place for me." At this time, she was the director of the alternative school, but she "didn't have a parish connection. So, they would not take a single woman as a volunteer, I couldn't find places to do the kind of ministry now I define as ministry work, I couldn't volunteer in the schools." She couldn't do retreat work and couldn't do any of that because she wasn't a nun, and "they did not have much acceptance of single women."

Pharmer maintains she learns about which direction to go through prayer. "Through prayer and through working with a spiritual director, it just became clear to me that I was called to go to seminary. So, then I decided, I investigated, uh, different churches, Lutheran churches in Milwaukee and found a church that was Central City that did a lot of community ministry and began to go there, and then I went to seminary after that."

She shares her learning experiences in deciding to enter seminary. "Well, I'd always done a lot of reading in theology, a lot of reading in Scripture and many of my friends went into advanced theological study or advanced Scripture study, and so I'd have lots of conversations with them". Pharmer discusses learning experiences through relationships. "I had friends in seminary, even in the Lutheran seminary, and so it was part of my social life, you know. I also

did a lot of work, social justice work, and so it was putting
that through the lens of my faith that was really part of my
learning experience."

Pharmer finds learning in seminary quite exciting and challenging. Her seminary is part of the "graduate theological
union in Berkley. So, there was a consortium of 11 seminaries, and that was fabulous, uh, because I was able to meet
so many people from so many different denominations."

At the same time, it becomes difficult for her because when
she went to seminary in 1982, there were very few women
in her class. "I was the oldest person in my class, so it was
all these young men who had had no experience of life. You
know, they went to college, and then they went to seminary,
that's wonderful, but it was very difficult for me, uh, in the
Lutheran seminary, and so I really found lots of connections in the larger seminary world." Though she experiences learning through reading and writing papers in seminary,
her perception of the church was different "but it was just
not in lots of ways the way that I saw the church." She feels
"there was a lot of competition, there wasn't much collaborative work, and it was very difficult as a woman. There
was one-woman faculty member, and she's younger than I
am. So, it was really hard. I don't think it's that way anymore, but it was a difficult experience."

Learning Experience in Spiritual Roles
Pharmer describes her learning experiences after seminary.

> Well, I very much appreciate the fact that continuing
> education is built into the relationship that I have in
> my contract with the congregation so that I have time
> and finances to do that. I've had some wonderful
> experiences of more in-depth Scripture study and then

that might be for a week at a time and then day work shops here and there a couple of days.

These learning experiences influence her ministry. "I'm also involved in the Sinsinawa Dominican community that is the religious order of sisters that I'm part of their anti-racism training team. So, that's been a five-year process that I've been involved in, and it's with that congregation, but it definitely influences what I'm doing here and how I'm working here. So, that's a lot of the study that I've done, and that's, so it's on a social level but looking at that through the lens of faith, particularly injustices or the racism in the church and to work in ways of dismantling that."

Pharmer discusses a significant learning experience that helps her meet the demands of her spiritual life. As a single mom, she claims living with her two children born in Haiti is an incredible learning experience.

I adopted my son when he was an infant, and I was married at the time. I got divorced and then I adopted my daughter who was almost four. So, learning about Haitian culture, living with two Haitians, even though they're U.S. folks, you know. As a friend of mine says, 'scratch the surface of my daughter particularly and she's Haitian all the way,' you know. So, there's, it's just been a cross-cultural experience for me as a mom to learn how people process and how they, how they come to decisions and how they communicate. There's all the other stuff of music and food, but there's this other way that people just process things in a way that is not familiar to me, so I had to learn how to do that. I think everybody has to do that, even with the biological children. You're like where does this kid come up with this? You know? But it's very significant for me because my children have a different culture than I do.

She believes dreams come to her as learning experiences which help her meet the demands of her spiritual life. She alludes to the text in Matthew for her Sunday's sermon where Joseph has the dream and Mary is pregnant. Pharmer asks-

> What is going on here? As a single parent, I relate to that perhaps differently than someone else, uh, as some one who I really believe in the power of dreams. And that's dreams and prayer and analysis of that is how I came to moving from the Roman Catholic Church to seminary and the Lutheran Church. So, all of that is very much related to my own experience, but I think my lens, my hermeneutic, to use that word, is different because of the home I live in and the children I am with and what they've brought to my life.

Pharmer identifies a particular challenging situation in her professional practice and describes how she learns to prepare herself for such a spiritual ordeal. The first thing that comes to her mind is the...

> difficulty that is so prevalent at this particular moment in the United States, this particular conflict that we find ourselves in and I think that has been an ongoing time of conflict in this congregation that I serve, but it's been in my whole professional life in the church that I would see conflict as not a choice for a Christian.

While she thinks armed conflict is not a choice, her experience with the Sandinistas poses a challenge to her.

> Armed conflict as not a choice? That was very

interesting to be with Sandinistas and to hear them say they felt that was the only thing they could do. So, that challenged me a little bit, so I don't think I can call myself a pacifist in the complete sense of the word

She feels the congregation is going through many difficult times. . . "Uh, it's always a stretch for me to listen and to hear people who are on the flip opposite side and to realize that I need to be pastoral as well as proclaim what I believe is the prophetic stance of the church. So, that's, always really hard. So, that's led me to prayer in a deeper way than I have ever been before." She establishes a very deep pastoral relationship with this small congregation and "feels her pastoral connection very intimately." So, she wants to be with these people as they're dying, and to be with them as they're facing trials, and "when we have a conflict and I don't want to just call it a political opinion because to me it's a faith issue, that I can't have that to be a gap, you know? So, this has been just an ongoing work with me all along."

Pharmer meets with her colleagues as a support learning group.

> I have a group of women that I meet with, women pastors. We call ourselves the pancake women because we meet at the Pancake House. Then I have also tried to be in connection with other Lutheran pastors through tech studies and through meetings, and even though we might not necessarily always agree, I find more meeting in agreement there than I find in the congregation, even though many, many people have come to this congregation and have expressed the reason why because of the city ministry and because of the activism of other people and

myself in justice issues.

She discusses ways in which her faith or beliefs help her create learning experiences toward her spiritual life.

> Uh, I try to do my teaching when I have Bible studies, with adults or children, in a way that connects their faith life with the Scripture story. For example, if the story is about the bent-over woman, you know, who reaches out for healing from Jesus, to talk about where are the places in our own lives where we are bent over, where we have been abused and then to take it to the community where as a community, are we so bent over that we can't see each other or so bent over that we have considered a way of life, racism again, or economic disparity as that's just the way it is. How, then, can the healing touch the challenging touch from Jesus in justice cause us to look up? That's kind of how I would do things. So, that's really how I approach teaching, preaching.

Pharmer speaks about another kind of learning experience.

> Well I'm an experiential learner. As I said, I don't start with a book and then go meet folks. I start with hearing what people have to say, formally or informally, and then I go to do the background reading or investigation or more formal learning of it. I love movies and fiction that's helped me a lot, particularly with people whose experience is not my own. For example, people who are gay and lesbian, it's not my experience and so I really learned and then I try to do reading or people who are alcoholics, either in recovery or still struggling with the disease. I've had to learn from them and then do more learning.

Integrating Secular and Spiritual Learning Experiences for Parish Ministry

She explains how connection with nature helps her integrate both her spiritual and secular life to meet the demands of her clergy roles.

> You know, I think I could say that connection with nature does that for me. I don't have the financial resources to do a lot of other experiences, you know, that's just not what's happening with my family right now, but I try to walk, I try to be at the lake. My children and I usually go to Door County at some point in the summer, but even though I live in the city, I live across the street from a community garden, a huge, one of the largest community gardens. So, I think nature rejuvenates me. It gives me energy and is also part of the rhythm of nature its part of the rhythm of God's renewal. I think that helps me.

Pharmer speaks further about integration of secular and spiritual lives

> Secular, really, I don't see a lot of division between my secular and my spiritual life. It's very integrated for me, it really is, or even what I do with my money, where I spend, uh, my money. I try really hard not to go to the mall you know what I mean? Here we are in the season of shop, shop, shop, and try to make alternatives to how we do those celebrations that are, uh, respectful of people's labor and work, and I think that comes from my spiritual and secular life being integrated.

Yet, she desires an integrated life. "Yeah, and I think I would like it to be. I work on having it being more integrated. I want it to be more of a whole and a part than I do this here and this over here kind of thing". Pharmer aspires for more opportunities to really be in situations that other people would label purely secular.

> I have no connection with the University, I have no connection with business except through congregation members, uh, and so I wish I could sometimes go places and be anonymous so that I could hear more or just be an observer more of what people call secular even though I would say God is connected, God is present. There are ways in which we are all connected that I call God. Uh, I had a, yeah, I think that's a struggle, that's a challenge for us or even to go through these questions you've given me a different thought process here, so I appreciate that.

She explains how the integration of her secular and spiritual lives influence her learning. "I think when I try to live and practice in the presence of God, that's then when the distinctions fall away. You know, there is a point when I am professional and on, you know, and I have to be listening attentively and be some way processing so that I can respond or doing administration work and that kind of stuff. There's also a time when I just need to sit in silence, and that helps me integrate the other stuff, you know"?

As a member of the Dominican community she engages in contemplation, a process that intersects the physical and the spiritual and from which learning emerges. "I was part of their overall model or overall way of life that is to contemplate and give to others the fruits of your contemplation. So, I know that within me there is more of a need for contemplation, for a way of looking mystically at the world than there might be for other people. That's just how

I got wired, you know? So, that's what I'm looking at all the time."

Pharmer claims secular life or spiritual life experiences must be analyzed.

> My kids will say to me when we go to a movie, 'can't we just go to a movie? Do you have to find something in it?' and I say, 'yeah, I gotta, we gotta analyze it, we gotta discuss it, you know, we gotta look at the under lying.' I can't just let it flash through my brain. So, in one sense I'm never turned off, you know, and in an other sense I have to have my time of interior reflection. It doesn't always have to be alone. It can be in community, too.

She focuses on technology and examines how that integrates learning for her growth. Yet, she thinks there are difficulties with the use of these gadgets:

> One of the things that I think about all the time is all of the gadgets that I have in my home that make instant gratification. The microwave I have my coffee pot programmed so that I get up in the morning and my coffee's ready. You know, I can cook. I have not fancy stuff, but I have it very convenient. On one hand, it makes things a little easier for me as I'm trying to make my home and provide a home for the children and hospitality for others.

> But it makes me impatient, you know? If it's not done in 10 seconds, I am just irritated. If I have to wait for the water to boil, what I try to counsel myself to do is to use that experience or use that as a way of saying, you know, 'that's not God's time…I think the car in

some ways can be a tool of the devil because it makes us go, go, go, go. It isolates us. You know, of course, there are a million convenient things, but it keeps us from feeling the cold and the heat and the snow and the rain and the ground. So, I very often try to be conscious when I use something that's external, a machine. I'm not a computer person, I hardly know how to operate it. I can't program my VCR, you know? So, I try to use those things wisely. Someone said one time in talking about how to live a simpler life to not have more than we can caress. So, it's okay to have a television, but do you need three televisions? You know that kind of thing, to realize the value and to be conscious of that.

Learning Opportunities and Professional Growth as Influenced by Gender and Position

Pharmer claims her gender and position make her stronger as she looks back from the administration of the church to preaching and seeing it through her own experience as a woman.

Very early on, I learned that women who are strongest… and I would call it feminism and I embrace that title and that's fine with me. Some people don't like it, but I do - those who are clear about their feminism have an easier time because we're just more out front and forthright which doesn't mean easier, doesn't mean I don't have conflicts and doesn't mean I haven't seen sexism in the church and all of that, but I try really hard to be authentic and this is the integrated part again, to just be authentic about it. Yeah, but it is a constant challenge with both men and women who are not still used to a woman having a position of authority particularly in the church: just being what you are or who you are? And not being afraid to use my voice. I try not to play games. If I have a position of authority as pastor in this church, I try to empower people, I try to have mutual ministry but, sometimes it comes down to the fact that I have to articulate a position, I have to articulate a matter of faith or it has happened also often where people cross the boundaries and are disrespectful to the community, and it comes down to me to call that to their attention, sometimes even to the church counsel's attention, and that's hard, that's real hard.

Pharmer defines learning experiences as interior reflection and communion with God.

CHAPTER FIVE
Pastor Lin Grace

Lin Grace serves as the co-pastor of a Presbyterian Church for the past four months. New to this Midwestern congregation, she is in her mid-forties, and has ministered in other congregations. "This is my fourth parish. I served in a church on Long Island in Bridgehampton. I served five years as co-pastor and then one year as solo pastor, and there were 275 in that congregation." Then she served in Bernardsville, New Jersey, outside of Morristown "near, not far from New York, it's kind of across the river." The Presbytery asked her to serve in this position because the church was in crisis at that time.

This congregation was of ethnic minorities and they had boomed in the 1950s and when their pastor had retired, they had gone from almost 500 members to 12, and the Presbytery wanted to see if that was a viable congregation, and by the grace of God, in the year that I was there we were able to increase and enhance our outreach to not only the ethnic communities but also the neighboring communities, and the ministry continues there, what it was in the 1950s, but it's about 100 so, feel good about that and so do I.

Her last position was in Cooperstown, New York, "an old congregation established in 1800, uh, and that was about 180 members, and I served as co-pastor and then a year as pastor".

Learning Experience in Secular Roles
Lin Grace started working at the age of 14. "I worked with the Glendale YMCA and I was a teacher for developmentally challenged and physically challenged children ages 2 to roughly 7, some were chronologically older, but emotionally and mentally about 7, and I worked with them. That was not a paid position but I volunteered for four years." She declares her learning experience from previous work was an asset.

> I used that experience, I was a day care supervisor for a year for a Hispanic day care, and this was in east LA. Then, I worked for a year as a program director at a detention for juveniles working with those that the social workers felt were most likely to be able to re-enter in a healthy way into community, and so I worked with them one night a week on their strengths and growing edges, mostly how to overcome, uh, that anger and that edge and that's what I did. I loved it.

Shortly, Lin Grace becomes aware of her strengths and a distinctive direction for her life. "I realized at that point that I liked working with children I liked working with youth but my passion for God and the church, I wanted to connect those two, and so when I began my formal education at the University level I was a religion and psychology major." She thinks, "being raised in the tradition where women didn't serve in the churches was a challenge" that must be overcome.

Lin Grace discusses a critical learning experience in her secular life that informs her daily life. "About three years ago I got 'mono' and it was a humbling experience because I couldn't do what I wanted to do, I'm a very active person, and the doctor put me on bed rest for a month. The kids who got it in the church, they were up in two weeks, but being the older person, you know, it took me a month." This is a countless learning experience. "I learned from that the importance of balance and taking care of a whole being, both in terms of our health, in terms of our physical activity, in terms of recreation. I love the church, and I would just pour heart and soul continually day and night into the church but realized that that wasn't good because, you know, as human beings we need to care for our whole selves, and uh, it was a humbling experience, it was very good".

Learning Experience in Transitions
Lin Grace speaks about her decision to enter seminary:

As I mentioned, it was a very big challenge. I came of age in the late 60s, early 70s, and at that point the ordination of women was still very new in the Presbyterian Church. We're celebrating our 50th year, as you know in 2006. Uh, and the biggest influence for me was in my University, I had a course on the book of Genesis and the course was very challenging and we had to give oral presentations once per week.

She describes her learning experience with a mentor as she wrestles with the decision to enter seminary.

The professor after one of my presentations said uh, 'you are going to seminary, aren't you'? And I said no, and he looked down upon me and took my hands and he said 'don't you dare keep closed a door that God is trying to open'. Uh and he was a Lutheran pastor and I was the only female in that class. There were all other male students, and so we talked about women in the church, and we talked about Paul's theology and we talked about the secular, uh, I'll use the word prejudice against women in those teaching roles, and I said, you know, I wasn't sure that I was good enough, and uh, he said it wasn't about being good enough, it was about being available for God's work, and he was wonderful because it took me three years to decide. I went into non ordained position in a church for two years after University, and he kept in contact with me as I prayerfully discerned if that was what God wanted me to do, and uh, what I did was finally at the end of the third year I said 'if God wanted me to, I would re search the seminaries and apply to one, and if I got in, then I was meant to go,' (laughs). That's what happened, and I went to Princeton.

Lin Grace says, "I loved seminary I just thrived on what was available to learn, both from our inheritance of the past, you know, all of the theologians we read and the studies and the method and methodologies, uh, I loved all that, I loved all that but I really appreciated the interaction with other students. Being more of an extrovert you know, I was very involved in my seminary at that time uh, and I took a position, a paid position as a deacon for the chapel which allowed me to uh, put together worship services and work with the minister of music and also the chaplain for coordinating worship at, uh, Princeton Seminary, and I loved that".

As deacon of the seminary chapel, she explains her learning experience. "That was just a rich experience, I learned a lot because there were some from not only conservative churches but also churches from around the globe that still had…and there are still churches here who are struggling with the ordination of women." she did not see herself as a "threatening person," but even when people were threatened because she was a woman in leadership, they "would talk about it, once people got to know me, that kind of exchange I think breaks down many of our prejudices, and so that was a real learning experience." Learning also occurs through sharing of different cultural perspectives.

One of my closest friends was a gentleman and his family from Ghana. His name is Reynard Smith, and he went back, he went back to be a pastor and we just loved it because he was from his tradition and his perspective, and I was from mine, but we were and his wife too, and his little girl, we just loved the exchange and the sharing and realized we had so much to learn from one another that really was a benefit and a blessing to my seminary.

Learning Experience in Spiritual Roles
Lin Grace continues to learn after seminary, reading different book genres. "I continued, even that first year of… I really enjoy reading and so I would read for my own benefit books of theology, books of pastoral care". Also, she learns through continuing education programs.

I regularly attended… I don't even keep track anymore, I stopped after about 20 courses of learning for continuing education within ministry. For my early years I focused a lot on preaching I was a preaching major so I wanted to focus on that". In later years she began to focus on spirituality. "And, continuing now really this passion within me of how to be spiritual leaders within our local congregation. I think in our country and our world people are starving for, yearning for more of a spiritual connection to God and to one another, and what we in western society have created are these pockets of isolation and we don't have those bridges of trust as readily even within the church and I think that that's hurting us as communities of faith, and what I want to explore, and I'm continuing to explore through my education, uh, there are opportunities for that.

She speaks about the different types of experiences that enhance learning in her life "Uh, my parents' divorce was a big one in childhood because uh, in the 50s and 60s, divorce was a sin and being a child of divorce there were people who couldn't play with me because my parents were divorced, and that kind of prejudice, you know, as a little girl I didn't get that at all, but it really helped me to see how judging others breaks down community."

Her experience with Scripture has also been a great learning experience. "Scripture continues to guide…the spirit continues to work within Scripture for our contemporary age, and so that was a real big one".

Frequent relocation is another type of experience that leads to learning in her life.

> Also, I would have to say, moving so much. The move to this town was the 20th move in my life, that was a lot, and so I went to eight elementary schools in those five years and I had to learn to get along with other people and learn that all people are valuable for who they are and in some of my schools. I was the minority, the Caucasian, some I was in the majority. Some, you know, uh, some English was the primary language, other times it was, uh, Spanish, and I grew up in LA. So, those

were all big learning experiences for me.

Lin Grace discusses an especially significant learning experience and describes how this experience helps her meet the demands of her spiritual life. "That would have to be the Academy for Spiritual Formation which is a part of the upper ministry in Nashville. I just finished a two-year course and there were 57 of us who covenanted to meet four times per year for one week and we followed the Benedictine model of the day, and twice per day we had presenters sharing with us anything from New Testament theology to social justice and it was fabulous. Learning occurred most through group interaction".

> But the strongest part of that for me was the small group I was a part of. Everybody had to be a part of one, and I think in ministry we are often afraid to be vulnerable with others because we had to work with them or leading them, they're our bosses, and all of those dynamics were taken out, and this was just a common sharing, and that was really a very good experience for me.

She attended her first course in San Francisco and will do a follow up course. "Starting in April, I have been accepted into that and that will be Nashville and that's another two years to keep growing". Lin Grace identifies a particular challenging situation in her professional practice and describes how she learns to prepare herself for such an ordeal.

> I would say one of the most challenging situations for me as a pastor was just about six years ago on December 18 an elder and trustee of my church committed suicide in New York. I had just come home, I had taken my children Christmas shopping, and the phone rang, and the spouse said, uh, 'he's dead.' I was the first one she called

and before she called the police, before she called anybody to help her. I came to the house I was the one who
called the police and the coroner, and I filed the report,
and so I was dealing with the legal issues but also
dealing with the spiritual issues of this woman who just
lost her spouse of 47 years through a violent event in her
home and all of those, you know. Where's God in this and
why now, and Christmas is coming, and he had grand
children and children and being a pillar of the community
and then the next day it was Christmas Sunday so that was
a really off the chart challenging weekend.

Lin Grace speaks about ways in which her faith or beliefs
help her create learning experiences concerning her personal and spiritual lives. "Everything I do. Uh, I can't, I can't
really separate my faith from my personal life. My faith and
my love for God and for people aren't separated from who
I am. That is who I am, and whether I'm in church praying
or walking my dog praying, I believe God is honoring those
prayers, and I look for opportunities to expand on that and
pray in different ways and learn from different people their
expressions, but my faith is not a part of me, it is me, that's
who I am". She claims learning brings about growth, so
she strives to learn at all times. "I think the more I serve the
more I recognize just how little I really know, and I always
want to be learning and growing and looking for opportunities to engage not only intellectually but emotionally and
personally with others so that I can continue to be not only
the pastor, but also the person that I believe God is calling
me to be"

Integrating Secular and Spiritual Learning Experiences for Parish Ministry

Lin Grace believes her role as a mother helps her integrate
both her spiritual and secular lives to meet the demands of

her clergy roles.

> I think the greatest learning experience was provided by
> my children because as much as I'm called to be a pastor,
> I'm also called to be a mother to them and to balance
> their needs as growing individuals with my passion for
> the church has been a huge learning experience. When
> they were younger, actually I took off four years from
> parish ministry because I just felt that those early
> childhood years were crucial, and I had something only
> I could give to them

She explains how the integration of her secular and spiritual lives influences how she learns. "I think what it does, it makes me open to all opportunities of learning, you know. Learning is not in a classroom, learning is not just in a church; learning can be on the street and in the supermarket, hiking, skiing. We can continue to learn and grow no matter where we are, what we're doing if we're open to God, using those opportunities for our instruction and growing edges."

Lin Grace further discusses the topic:

> When I'm with my family, that's not the same as
> ministering to someone who may be in need here at the
> church, that's different. The person I'm responding to
> may be different. I hope that the person I am responding
> to as a compassionate caring person is at least similar...
> that you would recognize that I don't change from
> being at church to being at home, except perhaps I relax
> a little more...

She explains the shift between secular and spiritual domains using grocery shopping as an illustration.

Sometimes the shifting would be more obvious than other times and in those four years that I took off, it was very obvious because I missed it, I didn't have the opportunities to study and teach Bible, I didn't have the opportunity to prepare a sermon. What I had to do was really focus on rocking my daughter to sleep... was sharing God's love too, and valuing that, although my passion was to be back in the parish which is what I ended up doing, but I don't regret at all that time with them because I felt that that was what I needed to do at that point.

So, at this point the shift for me doesn't seem that different it seems very subtle. You know, I went to the grocery store at my lunch hour today, and there was a woman at the cash register having a difficult time and I just talked with her ...I'm sorry she was having a hard day and she had a headache and I hoped her day would get better... but responding to her with the same com passion. I hope that if somebody came in that I would respond...although the situations are different, my internal sense of being is the same.

Lin Grace claims ministry is who she is. "I don't see ministry as a job at all, so when some people report to work, you know, I'm at work now and I'm a lawyer, I'm a doctor and when they go home, they're not those things. For me, ministry is not a job. Ministry is who I am, I am a minister, and whether I'm here at church or whether I'm at the grocery store or whether I'm watching my daughter play a volleyball game, I am a person of God seeking to love and serve God no matter where I am. So, ministry isn't something I do, it's somebody who I am, okay, sure." She perceives her spiritual and secular lives as a journey "and it's a journey, we don't reach our destination until we're on the other side to use that metaphor and so I always want to keep learning and always want to keep growing, and you know. I'll pick up a challenging book just so I can keep my mind sharp or I'll engage in, accept an invitation for maybe to share with people who think theologically different than I do so I can keep how is it for them? That's important for me to know if I'm going to be serving people, to know how other people are experiencing things".

Learning Opportunities and Professional Growth as Influenced by Gender and Position

Lin Grace thinks working in a male oriented field brings a lot of challenge and unique learning opportunities. "It is still difficult for women even though in the Presbyterian Church we've been ordained for nearly 50 years. Percentage-wise, males are chosen more than females, particularly in larger churches or in suburban city churches, small rural churches because men don't want to go there so that's a challenge." She describes specific challenges

> a couple of challenging things have been for me I had someone on the ecclesiastical governing level ask me if I had to go into ministry or couldn't I do something else and he was supposed to be an advocate for women in ministry and that threw me off. That was right before I was ordained. I was the first female pastor of this first church. That was established in 1670, and there were still descendants of the first pastor worshiping there so there was a lot of history.

She recalls her role as a co-pastor with a male clergy. "When he preached, there was this one person that took notes. When I preached, that person read a novel but I realized for me my way is not to confront but to continue to preach faithfully and I continue to respond to him pastorally, and by the end of the six years, he wasn't reading a novel so that was progress."

Also, she interviewed for a position for a solo pastor in a fairly large church, about 400 to 500 members and the PNC told her "we really, the pastoral nominating committee, we really like you, we like your gifts, but could we just look for another male to preach and could you do everything else and I said no, that's not going to work. Now that was in 1987, but still (1987) is not that long ago, you know, but those are blatant".

Lin Grace learns through spiritual connection with God and to one another, reflection in action- balance-self-care, health, physical activity, and recreation.

CHAPTER SIX
Pastor Clara

Clara, pastor in her early fifties of a Presbyterian Church
in the Midwest, oversees a congregation of three hundred
members. Seven years as co-pastor, Clara became the solo
pastor at the church. "After seven years when he chose to
leave . . . I became solo pastor the only pastor here. So,
I've been pastor, one of the pastors or pastor for 25 years."
Clara had no role models of women ministers during childhood. Her decision to become a minister was influenced by
her college friends. "The only jobs I had before I became a
pastor were secretarial"

Learning Experience in Secular Roles
Clara discusses a critical learning experience in her secular
life that informs her daily life. "I think being a mother is
a critical learning experience…my motherhood event has
been… I'm now into my 23rd year of it, so it's an ongoing
thing of learning not just how-to parent but as you know,
[you] being a father, we learn from our kids all the time."

Learning Experience in Transitions
Clara shares her learning experiences as she decides to en-

ter seminary. "When I was a child, I had no role models for women ministers. When I was a freshman or sophomore, I guess, in college, I took a basic Introductory to Religion class as one of the degree requirements and liked the class, so I kept taking more and more classes in the Religion Department. I finally decided I might as well major in it because I was taking all of my classes in it, but I had no thoughts of becoming a minister." Her decision to be a minister was greatly influenced by her college friends.

> During my junior and senior year in college, other people started raising that question for me and asking if I was going to be a minister, but with no role models of women ministers, that had not come to my thoughts yet, and I was also concerned that at that point I thought 'I can't solve my own problems, how am I supposed to help somebody else solve theirs?' and not realizing that my job as a pastor is not to solve your problems but to help you work through that, but I didn't understand that as a 21-year-old. I took the one basic New Testament class in college and the one basic Old Testament class in college and really loved those classes and wanted to study more, but they did not have New Testament advanced (laughs) or anything like that. Therefore, I started playing with the idea of graduate school.

Clara describes her struggles in the final moments of entering seminary. "A Methodist seminary was right across the street from the University I went to and the Detroit Presbyterian Candidate's Committee was willing to let me go to a Methodist seminary." So she entered the Masters of Divinity program and decided she would give it one year and if she liked it then she would pursue the program. "If I didn't, God didn't want me fighting, kicking and screaming all the way to ordination. So, I started the next fall after graduating from college, the next fall as a Master of Divinity candidate and after one or two days absolutely fell in love with it and nobody's been able to convince me to do anything else since then." She reflects on learning experiences whiles in college:

> Learning experiences were just being a major in religion, and I as definitely approaching it with my head more than my heart. I had a professor in college who was the first one to teach me that it's okay to argue with some thing in print. I grew up thinking if it was in a book, it must be right, it must be true, and I shouldn't argue with it. Dr. Cecil Franklin who was chairman of the Religion Department at the University of Denver said, "You shouldn't read a book unless you have a pen in your hand so you can argue," so he taught me how to argue with the great theologians which was something- a very foreign idea to me. So, he was a significant person. I would read extra books in the New Testament and Old Testament classes side books, and he and I would get into wonderful conversations in class and I'm sure drive the other students up the wall.

Clara describes her learning experiences in seminary. "I really enjoyed it. Uh, it was a long time ago. 'Describe my learning experiences'. I took the regular courses that were required obviously. Any extra courses that I could choose, I tended to gravitate toward pastoral care kinds of classes and counseling. Uh, I did not like Biblical Hebrew. Biblical Greek was okay, but Hebrew I didn't like, so I'm not sure what else…. Part of the learning that was most beneficial was the field education experiences. Well, I lived off campus a mile away, so it wasn't a long distance, but I wasn't on campus. I just remember the conversations around the lunch table or in the library or whatever".

Learning Experience in Spiritual Roles

Clara speaks about her learning experiences toward professional development "after seminary part of my call as required by the Presbytery is two weeks of study leave per year and a continuing education allowance, and I always take my study leave. I may not take both ... sometimes the dollars run out before the time runs out, but I've done a variety of... gone to a variety of workshops and conferences and those kinds of things as part of study leave. I also try to keep up with reading, but I'm not as good at that as many of my colleagues. I'm also a mom, so there's limited time."

Clara says, interaction with church members, and colleagues are among the experiences that lead to learning in her life. "The congregation here has taught me an incredible amount. I was trying to decide whether I should say more than I learned in seminary. It was a different kind of learning obviously but, I find that I learn a tremendous amount from the folks here and from hearing their stories and their struggles." She is on church committees, a learning experience she considers as continuing education. "Also, another continuing education kind of a thing is as I've sat on various committees in the Presbytery, that's also been a tremendous way of learning. I'm just finishing six years on the Committee on Ministry, and that's continuing education all the time." Clara describes an especially significant learning experience that helps her meet the demands of her spiritual life.

> I chaired the committee on ministry for two years, and that was definitely learning a lot about the church with a capital C and about churches with lower case c and pastors. It definitely affected my spiritual life because as

chairperson of the committee on ministry, I was privy to information that most other people were not, and the only way to get through much of that was through prayer so I found myself in situations that were uncomfortable sometimes and knowing more about my colleagues than I would have liked to have known occasionally. So, taking prayer walks was an important way of helping me process that.

Clara speaks about a challenging situation in her professional practice and describes how she learns to prepare herself for such an encounter. Difficult times for her are usually related around someone's death:

Well, having been here as long as I have, the congregation becomes part of my family and I their family. So, when I'm burying people whom I have known for 25 years, that's more difficult than burying someone who, you know, I just met a month ago, and I find the easiest way for me to get through some of those more difficult funerals is to do my crying at the computer as I'm preparing the sermon for their service, and then once I'm in worship, then I can lead the service with people still know that I knew the person. I don't mean to say that I lead it coldly, uh, but I can keep it together. So, prayer is a part of that. Uh, it helped me to lay aside my own personal and emotional connections with this person so I could lead the congregation and celebrate in the resurrection.

Clara talks about ways in which her faith helps her create learning experiences regarding her personal and spiritual life. She comments on the awareness in her spiritual life. "One of the things I've become more aware of in the last year is a need for my own time to connect spiritually and so it happens that also within the last year I've been invited to be a part of a small group of Presbyterians who meet over near Dubuque once a month for a spiritual guidance kind of group process event that I have found to be very, very helpful in renewing myself and helping me focus on where I am seeing God and feeling God's presence."

Integrating Secular and Spiritual Learning Experiences for Parish Ministry

Clara describes a learning experience that helps her integrate both her spiritual and secular lives to meet the demands of her clergy roles. She believes there are opportunities whether she is with folks in ministry setting or in other settings that would not necessarily be considered as ministry setting; like the grocery store. "There are four of us that meet regularly, it's a sharing time. The question behind it is always 'where have you sensed God's presence in the last month' or since we'd gathered last. Then the others reflect on what you say and then there's a prayer time and then we move on to the next person. So, it's spiritual guidance but not with one spiritual director but with four other people giving feedback."

Clara identifies differences between secular life and spiritual life which she attributes to the tension that often exists between the two domains.

> I know there is a difference, but I don't mean to give the impression that I'm a super spiritual person but I try to approach things from a spiritual perspective most of the time, so it's, so it's kind of a blended thing for me. Well, I think everything we do ought to be a response of God's love to us, so in that sense I don't see a separation, but when I go to the grocery store, do I think of that as a spiritual event no, I think I need to go get groceries, but I may run into somebody at the

grocery store from church or whatever, and I guess I'm saying I don't take off my pastor role very often.

She explains further integration of secular and spiritual lives...

> I think the congregation would say the person they see leading and worshiping on Sunday morning is indeed the same person they see at the grocery store or at the Laundromat or wherever. Maybe coming at it a different way a little bit is that I fully believe that God is with me whether I'm preaching on Sunday morning or doing the weekly shop at the grocery store, and that I am to lead the life of a Christian as best as I understand it whether I'm at church or at the grocery store, and I don't think of it as 'this is God's arena over here and this is the world's arena over there.' They're all interwoven in my mind.

Clara talks about keeping an eye and a heart open in every situation. This allows for a holistic life. "Being aware of God's presence and not compartmentalizing God, God is here but not here -It's all one big thing". She speaks about a vacation experience in Alaska. "A couple of summers ago we were up in Alaska and every day a different hymn would be going through my head just because of the sheer beauty of what we were seeing...that sense of wonder at God's creation not only in terms of the physical beauty of the world but also just the variety of people."

Learning Opportunities and Professional Growth as Influenced by Gender and Position

Clara understands that parish ministry is no more male oriented. "First of all, I'd say that, uh, I'm not sure it's a male oriented field anymore. When I was in seminary 25 years ago, 26 years ago, there were a third of the students women in the Master of Divinity program. Since then my understanding is it's well over half. Even though I was raised that the ministry was male oriented, I don't see that as much in the early 2000's that it's male oriented." She does not feel there are learning experiences she misses because of being female. "I think doors are wide open and I think within the Presbytery I've been given more than sufficient opportunities to serve at different levels in the church, and sometimes I might be asked to do something specifically because I'm female because those who are doing the selection feel that a female would be more appropriate in talking to so and so or such and such a person."

Clara learns through motherhood, small group relationships, and from the stories and struggles of church members. She seeks self-renewal through focusing on God, and feeling of God's presence.

Chapter Seven
Pastor Bonnie

Bonnie, pastor at United Church of Christ, located at the southwestern end of a Midwestern town is in her seventh year. "I'm the only ordained clergy serving this church with a congregation of about 200 members housed in a contemporary church building". In her late fifties, she has traveled extensively to Europe, Asia and the Middle East. Before she came to UCC she worked as the associate conference minister for 6 years with the United Church of Christ. Her responsibilities included women's issues, outreach ministry, and education.

Learning Experience in Secular Roles
Bonnie earned her undergraduate degree in elementary education and a master's degree in guidance and counseling. Her first job was in teaching. "I was an elementary school teacher, second grade for a number of years. Then I took a break and had children and was a stay-at-home mom for a while." She went back to school and got a Master's degree in guidance and counseling and then served as a "counselor in a senior citizen organization working with older people". Later, she got into educational ministry, not ordained

ministry. "And that's when I went into First Congregational Church educational ministry. My responsibility there was to organize, coordinate and develop educational ministries for children and their families."

Bonnie understands having children is a critical learning experience that informs her daily life. "It's having children that change your way of perceiving the world and your commitments and how much time you spend thinking about what the lives of the children are about." Another critical learning experience "would be the political situation in our nation right now which is disturbing to me. The conflict we're in is disturbing to me."

Learning Experience in Transitions
Bonnie speaks about her decision to enter seminary. It was a gradual process. "I think that it had to do with being in the church working with children and their families and realizing it was more than just about education. It was more than just teaching them about their faith, it was more about being with them in times of crisis and teaching the child involved, also being involved with parents, being involved with worship life of the family." Bonnie considers learning experiences she gains in seminary enable her to improve upon caring skills for both adults and children. "All of that came together for me, and it felt like I needed to know more in order to serve them better, so I went to seminary. I went to seminary to try to do a better job at what I was doing, and while I was there, I felt a broader call to do parish ministry and, in that way, affect adults and children as a pastor. So, I pursued being ordained at that point. I was ordained in 1991."

Bonnie describes her learning experience in the process of deciding to attend seminary. "Um … I did a lot of things before I went to seminary in terms of learning. I guess I was resisting the call to go into the ordained ministry for a while, and so I pursued other kinds of educational experiences." She takes a two-year class in Christian education, "Studying in Milwaukee for a couple of years, and that was great and wonderful.., but it just wasn't quite it. God keeps knocking on your door … 'Okay, that's not quite it, not quite it.' So, when I told my husband that I was going to go to seminary, and he said 'it's about time, I knew this was happening.' He could see it almost before I could see it. So, it was just gradual acceptance of what it was that I was supposed to do."

In seminary Bonnie's learning experiences occur through conversations with school mates. "Um … I went to seminary in Chicago. At that point, I had two children who were of school age here in my home town… so I traveled back and forth commuting back and forth to Chicago. So, over time I think just being in conversation with people in the seminary and I also kept my job in education at First Congregation Church. I think as I did both of those things, the more conversations I had, the more I was led to where I was going."

Learning Experience in Spiritual Roles
Bonnie believes learning after seminary occurs through informal group discussions. "We have a really good system In the United Church of Christ, especially in this particular area of the state of Wisconsin. After a person is ordained in the ministry, they're required to have an ongoing learning plan. It's pretty informal, but we're offered opportunities to get together with colleagues and discuss books." Also, she speaks about learning through continuing education programs. "In terms of education, when I worked for the conference office, I was fortunate in that part of my job was

to train congregations, but in order to train congregations to help them know about curriculum and about opportunities for ministries, I had to go and be trained myself, so I went to places." She traveled to a number of countries, a great learning experience. "As part of that job, I went to China, I went to Mexico, I went to Germany, and I went to Egypt. I had a lot of interesting experiences that I would then take back and help people figure how they could be connected with people around the world. So that was very good learning for me that broadened my understanding of the church from a local parish to the world." Also, Bonnie speaks about learning in workshops.

> I go to workshops periodically. Our church is growing and changing size from one way of being to another way of being, and I'm trying to be trained in doing that. I'm really good at being in relationship with people. I need to work on being able to pastor a church where I can't be in relationship with every person in that church because it has gotten too big. So, I'm going to a workshop on how to train leaders and they're the ones responsible for being in contact with all members in the church when it gets beyond the size where the pastor can do that.

Bonnie discusses a different kind of experience that leads to learning in her life; global awareness. "I think having more of a global awareness of the church has been really important for me. One of the things I've been doing lately is I've been connecting with Christians in Palestine." She went on a trip to Tantur Institute which is an institute of ecumenical learning in Jerusalem, and she was there for a month and she made some contacts in Bethlehem which is in the West Bank in Palestine. "This last summer was my sabbatical year and I had three months of study time opportunity, so I went back and stayed in Bethlehem and we have a connection now. My church and my association with Christmas Lutheran Church in Bethlehem so we are trying to support one another in our faith development and in relation to what the cultures are doing around us and to us and what we're participating in. So, I think the global piece is really important to me. And that got developed when I was the social conference minister in Wisconsin Conference of the United Church of Christ. I love studying. I love to go to school."

Bonnie believes another kind of experience that brings about learning in her life is educational programs for professional development. "I have a two-week professional development part of my contract, so I usually spend at least a week, maybe two going to a conference, or sometimes it's a week at a conference and a week reading on my own. I participate in association-wide study groups. I like the reading piece of it, but I like more the conversation with people around an issue or walking with people in their life. I'd rather go to Bethlehem than read about Bethlehem. But then after you have read, then you have to go, and then you read, and you know …" Bonnie describes an especially significant learning experience that helps her meet the demands of her spiritual life.

I think right now one might call me obsessed with our relationship with Christians in Palestine. That's been a significant piece of my faith development. Because of having been to the holy land, reading the Bible is much more alive. I can visualize places where stories happened or are said to have happened, so that has been really significant. Traveling to the holy land has made my reading a lot richer and deeper. Also, it's more the relationship with people who live in Palestine because of the kind of life they lead, the persecution they experience and yet the kind of hope they continue to have. It's not a hope based on reality, it's a hope based on the vision God has for us. That's real inspiring for me.

Bonnie's learning experience with the Palestinians manifests through her preaching and in her relationship with people. She speaks about how her relationship with the Christians in Palestine affects the work in her church.

Here, we have a small group of people who are responsible for our partnership with that congregation. Six of them traveled to meet me when I was in Israel. I was there for seven weeks. They traveled over there and spent two weeks with me and spent time with Christians of Bethlehem with whom we have partnership. So, they come with that excitement, too. Then, they went with me to our association which is 50 churches in the southwest area and proposed to have a partnership that involved more churches than just ours and the association agreed. So, now we have 50 churches that have some kind of connection with Christians in the West Bank, so I'm really excited about this. I see in them the kind of faith that is not limited by their circumstances. I think for us anytime we get discouraged, all we have to do is look at them and say 'wow, they keep going on, they keep believing that the world could be different.' Therefore, so should we. They've been more of an inspiration to me and us than we have to them, although the idea is we're helping them. We're trying to promote in the community and our nation what life is like for Palestinians because that story doesn't get told much.

Bonnie discusses a challenging situation in her professional practice and describes how she has learned to prepare herself for such an encounter. She believes the biggest issue for her and the congregation is that they live a pretty comfortable life and a pretty programmed life.

> So, it's hard, the challenge is for us not to let our lives take priority over our faith. I think that's my issue as well as my congregation's issue and the fact that we share it I think makes me a more effective pastor and preacher because when I preach, I preach for myself as well as for them what it is we're supposed to be about in life. I think the primary difficult issue is how do you make time in a very busy programmed life for that, and how do I prepare myself for that. I spend time talking to people and spend time studying scriptures and trying to read scriptures in light of the life that we have here and the life God intends for us and move us somehow closer toward the life that God wants and not the life we're necessarily living.

Bonnie addresses ways in which her faith helps her create learning experiences regarding her personal life and spiritual life, and she speaks about her reading habits. "Well, my faith has something to do for example, with the books I read, the books I pick up and the way I read them. It has something to do with the way I read the newspaper it has something to do with which programs I choose to watch on television and how I think about them. It has a lot to do with where I spend my time and where I try to learn that. I must have got seven books on my table in the living room that all have to do with Christians in Palestine. My faith has led me to read those. I wouldn't have read those if I had not had the experiences I had or felt the need to connect with people in that part of the world. So, clearly my faith decides for me about why I learned that. My faith creates them and drives them. For me it feels like faith has to be developed in a congregation, it's relational."

Integrating Secular and Spiritual Learning Experiences for Parish Ministry

Bonnie believes there is no separation between the secular and sacred. "I have to say it's hard for me to think about secular as separated from spiritual, but my experience in traveling to the holy land really did pull those two things together. She speaks about traveling as a way of integrating her secular and spiritual lives.

> I love to travel. Sign me up and I'm there! I would go on a trip every week if I had the money to do it. I would go somewhere interesting, exotic and unfamiliar. I like that. So, those kinds of learning experiences for me deepen my relationships and understanding of what it means to be human and how humans connect with God or who they call God, so for me the best learning experience is the travel experience. I went to China in 1995 and went to the World Council of Churches, the United Nations Conference on Women in Beijing. There were thousands of women, we talked about a variety of faith experiences what it was we thought our faith was trying to teach us about, what it meant to be a woman, and it was very similar whether women were Buddhist or Muslim or Christian or … our religion taught us some things about learning to be a woman and we shared those.

However, Bonnie perceives these experiences as "part sacred, part secular and it was a wonderful experience on how God speaks in a variety of ways to people through a variety of religious messages or belief systems." Bonnie reflects on her traveling experience and provides more insights about her ideas regarding integration of secular and sacred lives.

"Yes. I've been known to take trips that have not had much to do with faith. I've gone and lay on a beach somewhere on vacation, too. On the other hand, that's totally not faith either. God made this creation… the enjoyment of the beauties of creation is a pretty secular thing to do. On the other hand, if it weren't for God, they wouldn't be there. I don't see necessarily that there has to be a separation:

> The commercialization and sports activity of our lives, all of that separates us from God and from participation in the life of the church. I guess the challenge for us is not to see that as separate and to take our faith with us when we go to the marketplace or when we play sports or when we go to the voting booth. I understand there are people in this world who do separate secular and sacred and who do live a secular life who don't think much at all about where God is. So, it isn't that I don't see for example, travel can be a very secular activity. For many people, perhaps most, it is. But if what you're doing is recognizing God's role in that or connecting with people, trying to think of relationships, then God is there. So, part of my life is part of how I live my devotion to God, and sometimes I don't do that very well, but sometimes I do it very well. I don't see anything outside of that, so anything I preach the hope would be I'm learning it so I could be a better Christian or closer to what God intends. I have a friend who used to be my boss who, when we talk during breakfast, will always say when he sees it, 'that's your call.' So, I tend to do that and tend to interpret my life or experiences or inclinations in relation to what God intends for me. When I reflect on an activity, or a book I think it's impossible to separate what I think God wants from what I want. So, I think I take my faith with me everywhere I go, the way I approach life, read a book, talk to people.

She prefers moving away from self toward spiritual empowerment.

> It's easy to get too comfortable with yourself and
> feeling like 'I know what I'm doing, I'm good at it.
> So, I think until the world looks a lot different than
> it looks now, none of us ought to be too comfortable.
> I think my spiritual life, my relationship with God, my
> understanding of what God intends for all of us nudges
> me along. It encourages me to keep learning and not
> getting too comfortable.

Learning Opportunities and Professional Growth as Influenced by Gender and Position

Bonnie responds to the question about how her gender and position have influenced learning opportunities and professional growth. She begins by discussing the United Church of Christ as being the first denomination to ever ordain a woman, and that happened 1815 …

> a long time ago … Antoinette Brown. So, I am in a
> denomination that does in fact welcome women
> and I as a woman have less issues than some women
> in other denominations might have. Certainly, there
> are some churches within the denomination that
> have an issue around women but not this church.
> I am the first woman to serve in this church, but in
> the denomination, there's pretty much a welcome
> feel to it. So, part of what that meant was that my
> style of interacting was different than male styles of
> interacting. Although no one would want me to feel
> excluded, my style of understanding and articulating
> and seeing things was different. Sometimes I had
> to fight for my voice even among people who wanted
> me there.

She claims women now see "things a little differently and that over time women have quit trying to fit ourselves into a male role and have been encouraging women to become more comfortable as leaders. Women aren't all the same and neither are men all the same, but I think women bring to a situation on the whole a softer relational piece than do males. Male clergy tend to think it first, but we tend to feel it first. It doesn't mean men don't feel and women don't think. The first instinct, I think, and so I think one of the gifts we bring to congregations is our need and inclination to be relational." Bonnie speaks about challenges facing women. "I think congregations who are resistant to women are resistant because they think women aren't tough enough or aren't smart enough perhaps for the job. It doesn't usually take that long for that to go away and for everyone in the congregation to see 'this woman is challenging and it's also relational,' so I think it can be both."

When asked whether her role as a female clergy helps her in some way, she said "I have had to work hard and I've had to speak loud in order to be heard, but I haven't had as far as I can tell any times when I can't do something because I'm a woman. I have to admit I haven't had walls put up. I have had to work hard and I'm also the baby of the family and I've had to fight for anything. I was the only girl, so I learned to stand up for myself." She continues in her discussion regarding the issue of gender as it relates to her pastoral roles.

Every once in a while I will encounter someone who thinks my husband is the minister. People will call on the phone and be taken aback because I'm a minister. I don't allow it to intimidate me. So I think there's out there still some segment of the population that this is not an appropriate place for a woman. Because I'm in a denomination that doesn't believe that, I have some extra support behind me when I encounter that. So, I also have my own inner strength about this, but with the denomination behind this, I don't let it really bother me.

Bonnie asserts, there is still prejudice against women and it's the same issue here in the world in terms of race in the service of things… "We say where there's no issue and there is an issue! My son-in-law is African American and he says he always knows. So, it's not that everything is fine, but I think as long as a person has inner strength and also some support, then you can buckle up again for times when that happens."

Bonnie shares her perception about women. "I think women think differently and I think in terms of theology women have brought some interesting nuances to theological thought that in the past was thought one way and now we're saying it's not quite that way for us. So it's years ago, we talked about that, when women came into a bowl of soup they just kind of blended in and now instead of blending in we're going to stay the carrot or stay … we're not going to blend in and become a mushy cream of carrot soup. We're going to be… not blending in anymore. You can't be naïve and not feel the scriptural thing… gentle."

Bonnie learns through global awareness, visualization of places in the Holy Land and experience of God's presence, and connecting with people.

CHAPTER EIGHT
Pastor Bethke

Bethke, the solo pastor of a Methodist Church in a Midwestern town; cares for about 300 members. Prior to her appointment, she was the district superintendent a supervisory position responsible for 50 churches within the south central part of town. "I did that for 6 years, and prior to that I served 8 years as a lead pastor in a large 800 member congregation in Oshkosh." In addition, she served eight years as chaplain at a Methodist retirement center.

Learning Experience in Secular Roles
Bethke in her early fifties, holds an undergraduate degree in nursing. She believes her undergraduate work led her into the direction of nursing first, "Culturally I grew up on the farm and for kids graduating from high school in my age there were two options if you were a girl. One was teaching and one was nursing and I knew I didn't want to be a teacher so I went into nursing." She worked at St. Agnes Hospital in Fond du Lac while as a student and right after graduation "And actually that's about all I practiced full time in nursing, though nursing paid my way through seminary." Also she worked at Evanston hospital, in the closed unit of

the psychiatry ward and then at a Methodist Hospital "for a while. So, it's about 5 years fulltime and part time".

Bethke speaks about a critical learning experience in her secular life and shares how this learning experience informs her daily life. She recognizes that by gaining distance from things she is able to see God more clearly. She expresses this thought.

> Well let me start with yesterday's sermon and then I'll tell you how I live it out. Yesterday's sermon was taken from Hebrews chapter 11, which is about Abraham and Sarah, and the one that begins with, "Faith is the evidence of things not seen." You know, the assurance of things, so hopeful but not visible. And so I was talking about from a distance. You know, the scripture says they greeted it, the promises weren't fulfilled but they greeted the stuff from a distance. And so…I talked about how we gain distance from things in order to see God more clearly and that kind of stuff.

Bethke describes what gaining distance means. "And then yesterday afternoon I spent two hours out on the boat in the middle of Lake Mendota, and I said, oh, this is what it means, to get some distance, to get some perspective." She tells about another critical learning experience in her secular life that informs her daily life. "So whether it's… mowing the lawn, which is another of my learning experiences I write a lot of sermons on lawn mowers or, um, weeding the garden. Those are the places where I can get far enough away from the pesky details of things so that I can see the larger picture. And I may not even be thinking religion, God, or anything spiritual, but still, those are centering acts for me. Yes, and they inform my daily life."

Learning Experience in Transitions

Bethke speaks about her learning experiences in the process of deciding to enter seminary. She believes her involvement with the church coupled with her leadership roles brought about a significant learning experience. "I think I probably always knew I was called to ministry. It's just that it wasn't a question asked of girls in the sixties, and so because I was involved in the church, because I was involved in leadership roles, I started to see myself as being comfortable. Understand that I had some leadership abilities, and it actually was the sisters of the congregation of St. Agnes at Marion College where I went to school who probably helped me to discern my call into ordained ministry, which is interesting since they of course are not allowed to be ordained. And once I decided, I don't think that I had major struggles. It was fairly clear by the time I made that decision. But it was the experiences of learning theology and being comfortable with it, learning pastoral care, looking at the public speaking, at how one gives leadership in the church, and I continued to find all of those responsibilities comfortable."

Learning Experience in Spiritual Roles

Bathke discusses her learning experiences after seminary and how she continues to learn. "Important learning experience along the way has been my work with older adults at the retirement center. They probably helped me grow up. They pushed me to a depth of interaction, and of knowledge. They pushed me, because here I was, this young preacher, preaching to a bunch of wise, old people, many of whom were well known citizens in the city… And they cared about me, and they helped me grow up. Uh… that has been a major learning"… She speaks about another experience… "Another has been my work and my interaction with some of the other professional women in the city…, especially during that same time period, because I found myself better connected with the community, more able to be aware of community needs, and figure out ways of responding to those as well. Uh, and it probably also continued to push me. When you work in the middle of justice issues and socioeconomic questions, it starts to push on your own spiritual growth, and so those things were all connected."

Bethke explains an especially significant learning experience that helps her meet the demands of her spiritual life. "Okay, let me pull from another one because the one I just talked about would have been one of them. Uh, the other one was probably, oh gosh well there were two, I suppose. One was serving as the lead pastor for 8 years, and really finding myself in more of an administrative role and yet a pastoral role but recognizing the responsibility for seeing the larger vision, for keeping people moving, for resourcing people, for finding the spiritual gifts in others and bringing those forward." Bethke explains her learning experience.

> The most important lesson I learned is the one where the story they tell about the sign of a leader being one who brings everyone together to accomplish things and when the deed is accomplished and they looked at one another and say look at what we've done? And so my image of leadership and how I come to that is really that. It's never been important to me whether my name was attached to what ultimately happened but the joy is in watching others discover new gifts and abilities in themselves and actually accomplish things. So that was a major learning, and I had to learn that as a lead pastor because there isn't enough time or enough of you to do you find yourself orchestrating staff. The same is true with superintending because that is actually so much admin and personnel that unless you keep your

self very centered you start to think you're a pencil pushing paper…and that's not the case at all. So that was the other major learning for me about how to stay spiritually centered and offer leadership to pastors for whom I had supervision responsibilities.

Bethke identifies a particular challenging situation in her professional practice, and describes how she learns to prepare for such an encounter.

Um, let's take someone who is in serious physical crisis, 'cause that's easy for me coming out of my nursing background I've learned not to panic at the unexpected. I can overlook a thousand tubes coming out of a person anywhere. There isn't anything that I haven't seen, so I can't be surprised or shocked, I don't have to prepare for that part. Um, what I focus on is hearing where that person is. I've met people approaching surgery who were panicked, I've met people who were calm, I've met people who were in denial, and how do you find your way? So I prepare myself to be as open as I possibly can. I guess maybe I do think about what this person might want from me in terms of prayer, in terms of support. But until I've talked with, and we've gone through a conversation I don't know what that person is thinking and I don't know what's in their hearts. So I try to clear out all the garbage of my day when I meet somebody with a personal issue.

She describes how she helps troubled people find peace. "What I want to do is bring them to the most centered place they can be spiritually, the calmest place they can be. If there are unfinished pieces between families as they're waiting those things may have the opportunity to be said. Yeah, there is nothing I can do about the physical except that none of it bothers me, because I have seen most of it before."

Bethke speaks about ways in which her faith helps her create learning experiences concerning her personal and spiritual life. She speaks about an experience with a colleague.

> Long ago when I was a young clergywoman, and there were only a dozen or so of us in the United Methodist Church in this conference there was a woman who used to describe her image of God's kingdom as all people coming to a banquet table. So... and I've really continued to hold on to that one. She describes another learning experience. "And there is a print that I saw a while ago that I haven't been able to secure I think it's called "Sitting at the Banquet Table," literally and the ends of the picture do not have the ends of the table continues beyond the picture. And its people of ages, races, you know, languages, sitting at the table. So that really is a very helpful faith image for me. And so of course what it does for me is I just get really restless here, because we're so white ... We lack the color, the variety, and the racial ethnic experience that's really even representative of this neighborhood. So, that's a faith image for me, that image of inclusiveness that really drives a lot of what I, I'm always kicking people out into the neighborhood, and I just keep driving them crazy with that. Because they're missing, you know. So that's a pretty strong part of my faith journey."

Bethke examines learning in her role as clergy. "Formal education has given the framework. You know I didn't study liberation theology for nothing. Or process theology, systematic theology, all of the formal structures of things. You know, you learn formally the stories of Jesus and the stories of scripture, and yeah, they do shape you but it's the life experiences, it's some intuitive something that works with it… but I can't even describe it." She recalls her experience when she used to teach classes on aging.

And I would start by saying that I believe that all people are spiritual beings and that's the broadest definition I can come to. But, basically to understand that we are spiritual beings, is to say that we believe that there is someone or something, regardless of what name we give it that is greater than ourselves. And I think for those folks whether they're Christian or whatever, whoever they might be and whatever their belief might be, to believe that there is someone or something greater than ourselves immediately puts us in a different place than those who do not. But I think it has to do with the fact that when we believe that we're spiritual beings, we have taken a leap to say at some point for some reason we have committed ourselves, our lives, and our direction to the care of another. And that makes a difference.

Integrating Secular and Spiritual Learning Experiences for Parish Ministry

Bethke speaks about learning experiences, which help her integrate both her spiritual and secular lives to meet the demands of her clergy roles.

I think it's as simple as the moments when I've met people and without saying a word about religion or anything spiritual that there's something that's caused them to ask me the question about what is it that just made you say that or why do you think that way even though I may not be using a religious language. That who I am is strong enough representation to people that they catch a glimpse of something that they want to know more about. And I have had that happen just enough times with people that I say this is what it means to be in the presence of Christ in the case of the Christian church. This ought to be present enough in people so that as they go... there's something different about that person, and there's something that makes me wanna be a little more like them. Uh, so it's been those simple interactions, where someone says to me, "Why did you say that?" or "Listen, I've always wondered about that," or... that's not a very clear answer... but a lot of what I think is important and tends to come back to human interaction and relationships."

Bethke explains further what it means to integrate her secular and spiritual lives.

Not in myself I don't. I mean in me, whatever. The basic premise in my mind is that everything is sacred, whether it's religious or secular, by other people's definition. So, when I think secular and I respond to that I guess I'm looking at other people's perception rather than my own. See, I think they are one. I think they are integrated. It is not something that I leave here and I pick up again the next morning. It's a part of who I am, not only being clergy, but also being Christian. And my spiritual life is something that is a part of me and influences how I see everything including the kids I wave to when I pass... I back out of my driveway carefully, because I know there could be as many as 17 little kids in the circle playing. Um, I'm just aware of human life and respect. I don't put names on those things but they are influenced by who I am in my own faith journey.

She gathers insight from her grocery shopping experience.

"It's a really hard thing to describe, but I mean, you make me think that yeah, I don't go grocery shopping without being aware of efforts toward homelessness, or what are the healthiest things that I ought to be buying, because there is the stewardship of my own body, and care of that." Bethke relates integration of secular and spiritual lives to everyday life. "These little four-legged beings I have at home little lives, my little pets that there's sacredness about them. Uh, yeah, when I go to have my teeth cleaned I never do that without thinking about the, Harambe Dental Clinic and the lack of dental care in the city. I mean, that's a part of how my brain works."

She describes work being done by one group in her church to bridge the gap between the secular and spiritual lives of workers. "The other thing that I'm pleased with in this denomination is that we have an order called the order of deacon. And you may or may not have talked to someone. They are ordained clergy same status but their ordination is not toward sacrament, theirs is with a focus on word and in-terpretation in the world. So they help a person bridge what it means to work in a factory and to be doing something that's seen as spiritual. It's a very unique order of ordained clergy."

Bethke describes how the integration of her secular and spiritual lives influences how she learns. She then relates that to the connections that exist between people and objects:

It means that I wind up saying, now what's God trying to teach me out of this. I can't think of any simple illustrations. Uh, regardless of what happens to me in daily events, I'm more inclined to say, so what's the message here? And how does the learning connect me to my spiritual life?. . . and it keeps me I think more

open in my learning, more willing to live with questions..
. . less afraid to explore new ideas, or be accepting of
ideas that are… I'm still stuck in my own stuff, I'm still
limited by who I am, but it leaves me a little more open
to say a lot. I haven't thought about it that way before.
Because after all I believe God is steadfast, God is always doing a new thing. You've been helpful in identi
fying what I was trying to say. It really is, I can't pull
those apart, even make them different for me. And I
suppose that if you looked around the room here there
might be evidence of connectedness. You know, every
thing from the Doolittle's camouflage art which is
Native American to the places I've traveled and some
of the things I mean the world is always around me and
I insist that anybody else who comes in here be stuck
with my world too. Those are a part of my experiences
and I just seek to really remind people that the world is
larger than we think it is sometimes. And I don't know
how you separate the secular from the spiritual.

Learning Opportunities and Professional Growth as Influenced by Gender and Position

Bethke discusses how gender and position influence her
professional growth.

See, I've been in ministry since 1976. It's been awhile,
it's been 28 years. And, I remember when I used to be
the only woman in a seminary classroom. That's not
the case any longer, and I think that's a significant
change... there were some advantages given to me that
didn't happen to my brother colleagues. Uh, I don't
think that's the case anymore either. In fact, we joke
about it now because if you're a white male you're in
a lot of trouble. If you're a white female in ministry
you're in a lot of trouble, if you are African American

males in the United Methodist Church... When I think about… it's Muong, it's Korean, and it's Hispanic, so we keep moving through the list as people slowly increase in our ministry realm. There were advantages given to me as there have been to each of those subsequent groups because we look for the diversity, we grow the diversity, and this denomination is good at that. On the other hand, it is still true that sometimes a woman's voice is simply not heard, or heard in the same way. It's just, I am so glad to have the longevity ministry because that stuff used to really do me in. And it doesn't bother me anymore. It's kind of a test to see how long it takes from the time that I say something until someone else finally connects and go, "Well I think that we should do… "And no one remembers sometimes that it was me who said it two years ago. But it doesn't matter, as long as it's happening now. So I have learned patience and I have had to learn different ways of making things come to reality, because people don't hear a woman's voice in the same sense. Uh, I've had to struggle with the CEO image versus the pastor-prophet image. . . .and I've also had to struggle with my own… sometimes I want to set aside some of what I know are the woman images because I know they don't get the attention or the voice, and yet I know those are my strengths. And so I don't know how to describe it, but sometimes when people look to a leader they have a stereotypical image. It's tempting to fall into that in order to get things done. When that's not my venue and images the other is. Now, I can be stubborn and I can be autocratic. I learned those lessons well….So, I know those things but I really have learned to grow in some ways and be content that my mind may be somewhat, always seen as somewhat of a non-traditional approach, and that it's okay. They can live into it with me, and I'll learn where I need to make adjustments.

Bethke speaks about the need for some balance between women and men in the clergy profession. She hopes for a shared approach.

> First of all between me and laity because my role is really to empower and to instruct and guide laity so that laity can be involved in ministry. Second is that bringing together, and I'm probably more aware of it because it's not just male and female to me, it's the multiple generations, it's, I kind of look at all of those things. I look at the batch of youth growing up who offers everything from Spanish to German to Russian to French, and look for ways of integrating that. So I'm really very aware actually of when the leadership balance is more women than men. I mean, I yell when we've got more women involved in education because men need to be teaching men as well as women... I yell when trustees have too many men on them, because we need to have the balance. So I think I am probably very aware of that because of several reasons, one of which is that there have been articles written on the feminization of the church. Once the clergywomen start to go they'll take over and men will dive there the same way they dove out of education. They dove out of nursing and all that kind of stuff. So I'm aware of it. I'm also aware of the fact that all of us on one level or another have in us both components of maleness and femaleness, I simply do, and so it's helping men become comfortable with that expression of themselves so that talking about their spiritual lives is not wimpy stuff that they shouldn't be doing, but that they have the strength to be able to lead in that way too. And that woman can find those stronger traits in themselves that they might not always think are

there…."

Bethke shares insights about her experience regarding gender and position in relation to her clergy profession.

> Two other things that you made me think of. One is that I am aware that there still is a glass ceiling when it comes to how far clergy women can go and whether that's in salary… I really am one of the higher paid clergy women in the conference and so I'm aware that women struggle, and where we have what we would call clergywomen ghetto appointments, which means that we just put clergywomen there, and because we know the churches will take them, because they're either struggling or what not. And so I think we just created a ghetto, so we can just keep dumping clergywomen there. The second thing I'm aware of is that as the generations go by I'll look at well specifically I'll look at the Amanda Steins, She is probably 30 years old, fluent in Spanish and English, lived in Guatemala and several other places for a couple of years. Amanda provides a different perspective. She really does. She was just ordained an elder this year. But I look at her, and she is someone who continues to be aware of the issues, but I always worry that after some of us fought those battles, incredibly, that the next generation of clergywomen don't look around themselves and say well the work's been done, we've got what we need and we're there. I worry that without intentional efforts we'll continue to lose ground

Bethke learns by gaining distance from material objects to see God more clearly.

CONCLUSION

These women make various contributions related to growth as religious leaders through a variety of learning experiences. Three themes interconnecting their stories emerge. These themes broadly represent the central issues that empower them to engage in integrated learning experiences that inform their professional practices and help them meet the demands of their secular and spiritual lives. The three central issues are as follows: 1. Challenges in reconciling secular and spiritual lives; 2. Challenges in retaining a woman's voice in parish ministry; 3. Challenges in seeking self-renewal. The learning experiences these women attain enable them to address these issues.

Challenges in Reconciling Secular and Spiritual Lives
Women develop a learning approach to ministry through the integration of both their secular and spiritual lives. They emphasize how they infuse spirituality into their secular lives and thus, see their lives as spiritual, inclusive and balanced. Only a few offer examples of how they draw on secular lives to inform their spiritual practice. Women also define secular and spiritual lives differently. For example, some women consider secular life to be "time serving themselves" versus time serving others. Thus, integration

for these women seems complex and varying learning experience. In such learning events, they look for ways that are accommodating to their identities as women and to their individual need for self-renewal.

Challenges in Retaining a Woman's Voice in Parish Ministry

All the women carry memories of gender intolerance from the early stages of their ministry. Events in local congregations concerning other women clergy make them more aware of the existence of gender bias in parish ministry. Women wrestle with specific issues of gender. Some women speak about how they find ways of getting their voices heard. Other women give examples of their experience in parish ministry where some members of the congregation undermine their roles as ministers. There are those who also express concern about how more men receive a call to parish ministry than women. But resolving this issue is not so much of learning male roles as it is for them to shape their unique identities as women. These challenges bring about complex learning experiences; learning experiences that also offered ways for them to integrate their secular and spiritual lives and address their individual need for self-renewal.

Challenges in Seeking Self Renewal

Women become emotionally, physically and spiritually stressed when they engage in various learning activities to resolve the issues confronting them. Some women engage in renewal for holistic living. Other women suffer emotionally and spiritually as they interact with parishioners and seek unique ways for doing ministry. Finding a voice and trying to combine both their secular and spiritual lives pose great challenges for these women which call for self-renewal.

The stories reveal similarities in the learning practices these women demonstrate. These learning practices are interwoven across the issues that confront them. A closer look at these women's integrated learning practices reflects various learning models.

In many instances, these women's learning occurs through relationship. On the basic level, women stay in personal relationships and make new friends. They interact and make connections with friends and construct meaning on a personal level. Learning that occurs seems multifaceted and consistent with the literature on women's ways of knowing, reflective practice and constructivism. On the complex level of relationships almost all the women belong to multiple learning groups or learning communities where learning occurs constantly.

These learning communities are either located in groups of other women who are non-clergy or in groups of professionals including male and female clergy. These classifications sometimes overlap and often entail issues of faith. Because women participate in different learning communities and different learning groups, they engage in cross-contextual learning experiences that shape their identities and help them develop a sense of themselves as women ministers. Such learning experiences enhance understanding of local and global issues. Women also engage in dual contextual learning experiences or "gaining distance." It is the idea of temporal withdrawal from details of life to get the larger picture. For instance, women engage in gardening while simultaneously coming to understand gardening and God's purpose and greatness. In other learning moments, women engage in gender related activities like raising children and quilting.

On some occasion children become co-participants in meaning creation. In some instances, women experience learning when alone or engage in specific physical activities for instance, silence or gardening. Learning occurring from such practices is consistent with the reflective practice model as well as the personal constructivist perspective. Also, learning practices of women are consistent with learning transfer perspectives. Here, the learning practices seem reflective of women's previous secular learning experiences. An example is the transfer of learning from corporate America into the church.

These clergy women's learning experiences are not only mediated through rational thinking. They experience God in some unique ways and share stories about gaining new insights concerning themselves and their ministry.

Implications for Educational Practice

There are similarities in the learning experiences women have across the range of five denominations. The issues that enable them to engage in those learning experiences are typical of all the participants. For this reason, some implications for practice are considered.

Emphasis on Relationships in Seminary Education

For these women learning occurs mostly through relationships. They occasionally attend continuing education programs, but the relationships they develop are not sustaining. Women look for relationships that keep going and from which learning occurs constantly. Since there are not too many women clergy in the localities, they develop learning relationships with several women's groups. These women's experience with relationships begins in seminary. Seminaries should examine relationships among seminarians and help women develop this relational aspect of women's learning by encouraging group discussions in and out of the classroom. To continue those relationships, seminary women ought to be encouraged to become members of women's groups on campus and in field education placements. Women clergy in parish ministry may be invited to the seminary campus for ongoing conversation regarding learning through relationships.

Making Seminary Women Aware of Influences of Gender in Parish Ministry

Women clergy are still in the minority in parish ministry and that can sometimes be a difficult situation especially where there are not too many women to serve as role models. Seminary students both male and female ought to be part of an ongoing conversation that calls for holistic and inclusive parish ministry. The dynamics of power in gender roles ought to be discussed as well. Seminaries should invite women clergy occasionally to share their experiences of parish ministry.

Continuing Education Programs to Reflect Cross-Contextual Learning Experiences

Women belong to different learning groups and engage in cross-contextual learning experiences. They always learn in different situations. Designers of continuing education programs should consider such learning patterns. For example, workshops should be designed to incorporate different learning situations, such as in the context of preaching, context of silence, or context of societal issues. These cross-contextual learning experiences often occur in groups which are not necessarily affiliated with their congregation. So, local congregations ought to collaborate with various local groups in planning continuing education programs that serve the needs of the women clergy and their respective congregations.

Continuing Educational Programs for Reconciling Secular and Spiritual Lives

Women do not see separation between their secular and spiritual lives. They live integrated lives because they see everything as grounded in the sacred. In other words, they find God's presence in all events. Educational programs should reflect this understanding of women clergy's life experiences. A typical retreat program should include variety of learning experiences. There should be moments for silence. So, program participants should be allowed to find space and settle in silence for an hour or two. There should be time when participants may be allowed to participate for example, in a garden project. People may also do some artwork or knitting. When people sit in silence or engage in some physical activity, they construct meaning through critical reflection.

Continuing Education Programs for Self-Renewal

Continuing education programs should also emphasize renewal from physical, emotional and spiritual distress. Pastors should be allowed to identify and engage in activities that help resolve these stresses. Observing nature or hiking are good examples, which involve reflective practice and meaning making. Those activities then become learning experiences from which pastors gather new insights and new learning for ministry.

Continuing Education Programs to Reflect Clergy Issues

Issues confronting these women enable them to engage in learning experiences that inform their professional practices. Continuing education program designers should also consider issues confronting participants when planning programs for ministers.

Informal Learning Should Be Emphasized
Marsick and Watkins (2015) state that informal and incidental learning are relevant to practice in many institutions and
contexts. The findings show that these ministers learn always
mainly through informal learning activities. Informal learning should be encouraged among the clergy and the laity.

Church Institutions to Provide Space for Learning
Both ministers and the laity need physical and emotional
(i.e., solitude) space to engage in learning. Such opportunities should be provided to help them cultivate the orientation
toward learning.
Teaching and Learning
Learning experiences of these ministers reflect a co-teach-
ing-and-learning dynamic, in which they are both educa-
tors and learners simultaneously. Designers of continuing
education programs for clergy should consider the idea
of fostering a "participatory learning culture," a situation
whereby both learners and teachers become co-participants
in interpreting, teaching and learning the program. This
may serve to make the role of the clergy as learners more
visible and acceptable, as well as more directly, recruiting
the knowledge and experiences of church members.

Implications for Research
Women clergy stories in this book raise several questions
that require further investigation.

Spiritual Learning
Some women commune with God through prayer and
experience dreams. Their encounters with God reveal new
insights and new learning. Research to explore the nature
of learning that emerges when one encounters God through
activities like prayer or silence enriches the literature on the
subject.

Research Focus on Male and Non-Solo Women Pastors

These women solo pastors serve as head of staff. They can utilize all kinds of innovations in their day-to-day pastoral work. A similar research study with a focus on the learning experiences of male and supervised non-solo women clergy may provide interesting findings for comparison.

Denominational Study on Women Clergy Learning Experiences

These stories focus on five denominations which are unique in some ways. There are differences in seminary education as well as the ordination processes. The practice of ministry may also vary from one denomination to the other. A research study focusing on a specific denomination would provide additional insights on the subject.

Transfer of Learning from Corporate World into Parish Ministry

All the women once work in secular institutions or organizations; thus, they adapt their learning experiences into parish ministry. Only one woman transferred her learning experiences from the corporate world into the church. There are similarities between corporate management structures and that of church organizations. A research focus on learning transfer from the corporate sector into the church may yield some interesting findings.

Separating Work from Personal Roles and the Impact on Clergy Professional Practice

Some women segmented life roles from work. While some Christians may not welcome such practice, a research focus on the subject may shed light on how well clergy who segment work and life role perform under similar working conditions.

Silence in Adult Learning

Some women experience learning through the practice of silence. The practice of silence enables one to reconcile secular and spiritual lives. People aspire to live integrated lives; therefore, further studies in this area may provide an in depth understanding of the practice of silence and its affordances for learning.

References

Apple, M. W., (2013). Educating the "right" way, London: Routledge Falmer.

Dimitriadis, G., and McCarthy, C. (2001). Reading & teaching the postcolonial from Baldwin to Basquiat and beyond New York: Teachers College Press.

Merriam, S. B., Caffarella, R. S. and Baumgartner, Lisa (2006) Learning in adulthood A Comprehensive Guide. San Francisco: Jossey Bass.

Schon, D. A., (2017). The Reflective Practitioner: How Professionals Think in Action. London: Routledge.

Marsick and Watkins (2015), Informal and Incidental Learning in the Work Place. London:Routledge.